HISTORY

IN

Geographic Perspective

THE OTHER FRANCE

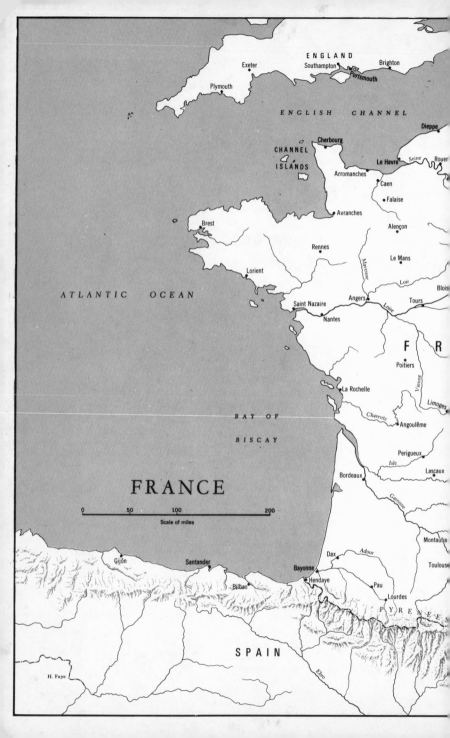

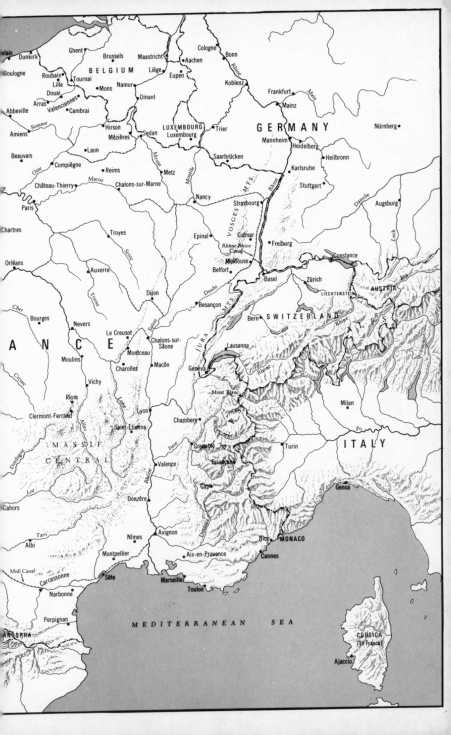

Other books by Edward W. Fox

OXFORD ATLAS OF EUROPEAN HISTORY, 1956

OXFORD ATLAS OF AMERICAN HISTORY, 1963

DEVELOPMENT OF WESTERN

CIVILIZATION SERIES (ED.)

HISTORY

IN

Geographic Perspective

THE OTHER FRANCE

———•———

Edward Whiting Fox

The Norton Library
W · W · NORTON & COMPANY · INC ·
NEW YORK

FOR E. S. F.

Books That Live
The Norton imprint on a book means that in the publisher's
estimation it is a book not for a single season but for the years.
W. W. Norton & Company, Inc.

ISBN   0   393   00650   6

PRINTED IN THE UNITED STATES OF AMERICA

1 2 3 4 5 6 7 8 9 0

Contents

————•————

Maps

———•———

Preface

———————◆———————

THIS BOOK grew out of direct observation of French political behavior. That it now presents a general, speculative hypothesis of historical development is due not to any original intention to theorize but rather to an inability to describe and explain French politics in existing terms. In 1965, I followed the French presidential campaign and, in the spring of 1966, the political revival it engendered, by attending conferences, meetings, and conventions in Paris and throughout the provinces. It had been my hope to elucidate some of the complexities and contradictions of French politics by viewing them in a historical perspective. To my surprise, however, the process worked in reverse, and at least initially, my political observations contributed more to my historical understanding than they gained from it.

I first realized this reversal in the spring of 1966, when, on succeeding weekends, I attended a national convention of the new Center party in Lyon and a colloquium of the new Left in Grenoble. Having first been impressed, at Lyon, by the character and quality of both the delegates and their discussions, I was astonished at Grenoble to find that, if the level of the performers was equally high, their style and orientation were quite different. Even while using the same words and grammar, the delegates spoke another language of ideas. They seemed to come from another world; and I found myself driven back, reluctantly but inescapably, to the old truism that there is, indeed, a second France.

Although the hypothesis that France has been divided against herself has long been widely held, I had been unwilling to accept it. My first research assignment as a graduate student had led me to suspect that it was not only historically indefensible, but had been deliberately fostered for ulterior political purposes. My best efforts to identify and incriminate the proto-fascist anti-republicans who, during the heyday of the dictators, everyone assumed had lurked beneath the surface of French politics before the First World War, proved unavailing. Royalism, I discovered, was an anachronism metamorphosed into a chimera by cynical politicians of the Left. Even if social snobs and literary *arrivistes* had connived at this political sleight of hand, I could find no solid evidence of the standard allegation that all Frenchmen were still divided by the Revolution, as the most famous version of the thesis ran. Instead, I came to realize that anyone of any consequence in France, from the Pretender up or down, owed his position to that same Revolution. Confusion, yes; schizophrenia, no.

Others, however, obviously saw what I could not; and after the Liberation in 1944, important new analytical studies developed the old theme. In 1946, Professor François Goguel published his *Politique des partis en France sous la Troisième République*. Far superior to any prewar study of Third Republic politics, it was based on a careful investigation of major elections and parliamentary votes and offered the conclusion that, in spite of the multiplicity of political groups, Frenchmen voted ultimately for "order" or "movement."

Although Goguel and his students have attempted to translate these *partis* into fixed voting habits within certain groups and regions, their success has been limited by their methods. Even where they find consistent majorities for or against "progress" in given electoral circumscriptions, they have experienced great difficulty in discovering rational explanations for these patterns. First, they can only assume that individual voters have remained faithful to their commitments, rather than switching positions among themselves to preserve a constant average; second, when twin villages or neighboring departments with similar conditions regularly supported opposite sides of important issues, they had little to offer by way of sociological explanation. In parliamentary votes, moreover, they had to account for the frequent shift of individual deputies, particularly as the debate moved from foreign policy or social intent to finance, recalling André Siegfried's famous aphorism that if a Frenchman's heart was on the left, he carried his pocketbook on the right. Ignoring the implicit suggestion that the line of political cleavage in France ran through the body of each voter rather than the body politic, Professor Goguel seems to conclude that Frenchmen tend to make political choices in terms of their own personal commitment to the *status quo,* thus dividing the electorate into *partis* of order and movement. Although he recognizes a tendency for those with most at stake to defend the existing state of affairs, he eschews any rigorous class analysis and tends to deal, instead, largely in moral terms. The party of movement emerges as a political version of Calvin's elect.

In another well-known interpretation, economic historians attributed the country's chronic resistance to industrial development to a special bourgeois entrepreneurial mentality. First advanced after the Liberation, when the urgent need of industrial modernization was widely recognized by economists, if not by the average voters, let alone the factory owners, this hypothesis was in fact a political indictment. Because the bourgeois preferred outright control of small protected industries to mere investment in large concerns—even if the latter would bring them greater wealth—they were held responsible for the country's economic stagnation. But even if the charge is accepted, the allegation that this was some characteristically French aberration did not stand up. Other bourgeois entrepreneurs (those of New England, for example) had exhibited the same perverse preference for personal control of their own small enterprises. The critical difference seemed to be that in France economic conditions had changed more slowly than in England or America and had thus allowed the recalcitrant bourgeois to survive into another age. In general, the exponents of the entrepreneurial hypothesis appeared to paraphrase Goguel's formula of "movement and order" and to see the problem ultimately in moral rather than economic terms. But if they too missed the clue that two separate economies shared the hexagon of France, they did not exhaust the possibilities of economic interpretation.

France has not lacked Marxist critics, but their economic

analyses have commonly foundered on the problem of correlating urban and rural classes. Obviously, few modern western countries have a more alienated proletariat or a more property-conscious bourgeoisie, large or small; but no simple theory of class conflict has ever served to organize political forces or to analyze political behavior effectively in France. Any simple Marxian approach is likely to lead to the conclusion that the country has suffered most from industrial underdevelopment and the consequent failure to produce a sufficiently large and aggressive proletariat to force the acceptance of a modern program of social reform. It has often been suggested that the peasants formed a caste, and the workers a class apart, but why the two found no common interests and became political opponents, rather than allies, has not received any generally accepted explanation.

A brilliant if eccentric version of the Marxist thesis was developed by the monarchist polemicist Emmanuel Beau de Loménie in his multivolume study, *La Responsabilité des dynasties bourgeoises,* which he began to publish in 1943. The great bankers, he contends, financed the railway construction of the 1840's and 1850's only to find their investment vulnerable to political authority. In this situation, he continues, they decided their best defense lay in controlling the state itself, which, he insists, they managed to do for a century or more. Despite the Marxian enthusiasm with which Beau de Lomenie denounces these capitalist villains, he reserves his moral opprobrium for the Orleanists among them, who defected from the monarchist cause to connive and cooperate with the *grands bourgeois* of the Center Left. His contention that the two joined forces to protect their common investments by joint control of the state stands up, but the charge of treason leveled against the Orleanists remains to be established.

That they felt more commitment to their substantial wealth than to an ephemeral monarchy, and consequently not merely accepted the Republic but actually cooperated with rich republicans in its management and defense, is borne out by the record. That they ever owed or acknowledged any allegiance to the Legitimist Monarchy, however, is another issue and one that

Beau de Loménie fails to join. Instead, he dismisses the Orleanist course as the product of rank material self-interest and the Republic it supported as an institution of capitalist repression. Only the Legitimist monarchy, he contends, could have saved the lower classes from the politico-economic exploitation of the bourgeoisie. This quixotic paradox recalls the Berth-Valois attempt to amalgamate the ideas of Georges Sorel and Charles Maurras and, like it, manages to reach neither the workers nor the Legitimists for all its intellectual flamboyance. But even if in its present form the thesis adds little to our understanding of either the motivation or alignments of political forces in France, some of its implications seem to correspond to certain recognizable patterns of behavior.

In arguing that the Orleanists used the Third Republic as an institutional defense of property, M. Beau de Loménie called attention to the similarities between that regime and the July Monarchy and thereby opened the possibility that it was the Republic that had become a monarchy, rather than that the monarchists had become republicans. Some time ago, when constitutional reform was an urgent issue, I recognized that political labels could be seriously misleading and attempted to classify the nearly twenty regimes that had governed France in modern times. Virtually all, I found, could be reduced to three general categories: parliamentary, administrative, and revolutionary. For most of the nineteenth and first half of the twentieth centuries, the normal form, whether labeled "constitutional monarchy" or "republic," was what I defined as "parliamentary." In the seventeenth and eighteenth centuries, however, as well as during important interludes in the second half of both the nineteenth and twentieth centuries, France was administered by either a monarch, an emperor, or a president. In brief transitional episodes between these major regimes, the French resorted to unicameral governments intended to reorganize the basic structure of the country, to rewrite its constitution, and to defend its existence. These institutions were called "republics."

Gradually I came to realize that these different types of government were used in different situations. Following the chaos of the religious civil wars, the French eagerly submitted to an absolute monarch in a desperate quest for security and peace. In return, they were well administered for a hundred years or more, but eventually they found their royal state incapable of effecting the necessary structural adjustments to changing conditions. Having recognized the gravity of their situation by the end of the eighteenth century, they then attempted to transform their administrative monarchy into a parliamentary model capable of political reform only to find that their difficulties had meanwhile grown to revolutionary proportions that demanded a constitutional convention. Once the country and its institutions had been ruthlessly reorganized, however, the French readily accepted the administrative rule of Napoleon and, following his defeat, gave a limited parliamentary government another try. Ironically, this constitutional façade was used by those who wielded the power behind the throne more to obstruct than to effect necessary changes, thus provoking two new, brief, revolutionary interludes. After order was again restored, the country returned to administrative government for the purpose of reconstituting the *status quo*. At the beginning of his reign Napoleon III used his great personal power to force the French across the threshold of the industrial age, but before the end he dissolved his essentially unlimited authority in a constitutional monarchy which, thanks to the Prussian War, eventually emerged in the guise of a republic.

Although this typology of regimes lent some coherence to my study of French history, it added little to my basic comprehension of its mysteries. Why did half the country's monarchists become covert republicans? Who were the republicans who alternately supported revolutionary conventions and administrative empires, but often opposed parliamentary republics? And what inner logic organized those distinct segments of the population that I, following so many predecessors, had finally seen with my own eyes? By his attempt to retrace the course of the Orleanists through history, Beau de Loménie had demonstrated that the critical division in French society did not follow the traditional dichotomies of Red and Black, Left and Right, nor even bourgeois and proletariat, but, instead, ran right through the middle of the monarchists. This made me wonder if some similar flaw did not split the Left and Center as well. For years the accepted pattern for analyzing election results or parliamentary votes has been sextuplicate: a Communist and non-Communist Left, a clerical and anti-clerical Center, and a parliamentary and anti-parliamentary Right. Was it possible that these lines splitting each major group were in fact continuous, dividing two separate political bodies each with its own Left, Right, and Center? Even if this hypothesis offered a simpler explanation of the legendary incoherence of French politics than the standard assumption that all Frenchmen were politically incompetent or perverse, what were its ultimate implications? Could it be extended to project the existence of two distinct societies in a single nation state?

For an American, it was natural to begin by seeking to identify these societies in sectional terms. The French themselves, of course, have frequently made sweeping generalizations about their regional differences, but they have never been able to agree whether the line dividing progressive from reactionary France runs east and west, or north and south. The problem is considerably complicated by the fact that the economically progressive east votes as enthusiastically for "order" as the backward west, while the underdeveloped south traditionally supports "progress." It would be necessary to go back to the Albigensian Crusade to find anything that could possibly be described as a sectional civil war; subsequent outbreaks of internal conflict have notably failed to produce clear geographical divisions. During the Revolution, Federalist opposition centered in the great peripheral cities, suggesting to some commentators the traditional opposition of the provinces to Paris. Yet, in this confrontation, Paris drew its strength from the Jacobin clubs of the towns and smaller cities scattered throughout provincial France. Could it be that the Federalists represented an external rather than a provincial opposition, a second France struggling to free itself from Paris and the internal France of the Jacobins?

It is certainly possible to discern the resemblance between the old administrative regime and the chain of communication and command that the Jacobins established between the capital and the provincial towns. Similarly, the concept of constitutional monarchy was unquestionably familiar to the Girondins and, through them, to the Federalists. Is the possibility of the Girondins surviving the Revolution to manage the Restoration and eventually establish the Third Republic worth a moment's speculation? What sort of social organism would this imply? What could explain its existence? And how could it maintain itself— let alone dominate the entire country? What, indeed, was the essential structure of these elusive but persistent groups? Could they be social structures in any meaningful sense, and if so, would they have developed, as Professor Lévi-Strauss has claimed primitive societies do, within patterns of the circulation of goods, wives, or messages?

Among those peripheral cities, half were ocean ports and, therefore, might once have participated in different patterns of exchange than were accessible to the smaller inland towns; yet surely modern systems of communication should long since have blurred any differences that access to the sea might once have made. Could anything of this sort have existed in the mid-nineteenth or mid-eighteenth centuries? And, if discrete social structures had existed within essentially independent systems of communication and exchange in preceding centuries, was there perhaps some possibility they still survived in a residual form?

In the eighteenth century most Frenchmen must have lived within narrowly circumscribed geographical limits. Rural towns and their satellite farming communities would have been at least as self-contained as many still were, following the Liberation in 1944. At the same time, even the most isolated were, either directly or indirectly, in fiscal and administrative communication with the capital. The port cities, on the other hand, participated in an entirely different system of communication. Their access to the sea gave them easy contact with all the other oceanic ports that made up the dynamic commercial sector of the pre-industrial world. Should this, however, imply that a city like Bordeaux belonged more to some maritime community than to France? The history of the city certainly revealed resistance to, and resentment of, the royal administration, and its economic record shows surprisingly limited relations with its hinterland. The possibility that Bordeaux, because of its access to the sea, was not a fully integrated part of the French monarchy seemed at once preposterous and intriguing.

If the two societies had developed in France along two different systems of communication, presumably their structures would coincide with patterns of travel and transport, following lines of low geographical resistance. If this possibility appeared to offer an explanation of the social dichotomy in France, it also raised a specter—the problem of geographical determinism— in a new form. Further, if such a hypothesis proved useful in analyzing French development, it should also be applicable to other areas. To be meaningful for modern France, this interpre- tation would have to work, with appropriate adjustments, for societies in other times and places and would, therefore, require the construction of a general theoretical base. In the first three chapters I have established categories, identified early historical models, and traced their development and extension from the ancient Mediterranean north to the Baltic and west to the Atlantic in the process that created Europe. In the next four, I have tested this theory and some of its corollaries in a systematic analysis of French history since the end of the *ancien régime*. In a final section I have offered some tentative conclusions and called attention to some possible implications of the general hypothesis.

Acknowledgments

———————●———————

Although this book was written within a period of two years, it is the product of two decades' effort to understand the complexities and contradictions of modern France. Because I attempt to resolve these problems by examining them not merely in a longer historical, but broader geographical perspective, the text reflects more or less consciously almost all professional reading or discussions in which I have been engaged during that time. As a result, it would be futile to try to acknowledge all my sources, and misleading to list merely those of which I was aware, except in a few specific and important cases. It will be obvious to any reader that I have benefited—even if indirectly—from predecessors in the wide range of fields on which I touch; but to attempt to cite such possible debts would risk being either pretentious or misleading. While I am more than happy to give credit to Marx, Weber, Polanyi, and a host of others whose influence my readers may detect between my lines, I should feel uncomfortable in leaning on their authority for conclusions that were my own. Moreover, because the manuscript was not constructed in the traditional manner from note card to note card, I have omitted the conventional footnotes and bibliography.

There are, however, a few specific and important personal debts which it is my pleasure as well as obligation to acknowledge. First, it was the late Major Thomas H. Thomas who not only called my attention to the importance of the geographical dimension in history, but demonstrated how effective a critical tool it could be. Without this introduction, it is doubtful that I should have discovered the path I have followed here. Second, it was my daughter, Elizabeth F. Genovese, who in endless conversations helped me develop my ideas and by the unstinted devotion of her professional talents—as an editor as well as a historian—made it possible for me to bring my project to a coherent conclusion.

Perhaps the effective starting point of this study was the seminar on modern France conducted at the Institute for Advanced Study during the fall of 1950. For the privilege of being a member of that group and of being invited to spend three more terms at the Institute, I am grateful to Edward Meade Earle, J. Robert Oppenheimer, and Sir Llewellyn Woodward, all now deceased. And for the financial support to make my stay possible I owe a debt, too long overdue, to the Carnegie Corporation of New York. The manuscript on France at mid-century which I drafted during my residence at the Institute did not seem to me to have a firm enough analytical structure to be published, and it has taken me the intervening twenty years to develop the one presented here.

To my many French friends and acquaintances who have welcomed me so often and generously to their country and their homes, I am obligated for far more than hospitality and personal memories. Their contributions to my understanding of France have been invaluable; but because it would be as awkward to name them all as it would be to cite all my academic sources. I offer them, collectively, my affectionate recognition in the name of the late Maître Marthe Huet.

Professors Eugene D. Genovese and Traian Stoianovitch read and criticized the manuscript with a care that saved me from innumerable errors. Mrs. Shirley M. Gruner, by her article "Historiography in Restoration France," published in *History and Theory* (Vol. VIII, no. 3) called Montlosier's *De la Monarchie Française* to my attention. The Velhagen-Klasing-Cornelsen Verlag granted me permission to use adaptations of two maps from their *Putzger Historischer Weltatlas;* and Professor John W. Reps supplied a print of the engraving of Philadelphia in the eighteenth century reproduced in the text. Mrs. Donna M. Schutz and Mrs. Janet S. Olesen typed and retyped successive drafts with a cheerful patience that contributed in no small measure to the completion of this essay. Needless to say, I alone am responsible for its inevitable shortcomings. This book is dedicated to my wife.

E. W. F.

CHAPTER ONE

The Geographic Dimension of History

HISTORY AND GEOGRAPHY were once assumed to be sister sciences so close in method and focus as to verge on representing two aspects of a single subject. Today they share nothing, not even regrets for what had been looked upon as a particularly promising alliance. The purpose of this chapter is first, to determine how this breach occurred and whether it was inevitable, and second, to suggest how and why it might be repaired. The conclusion proposed here is that history would stand to gain surprisingly from the proper reintroduction of the geographical dimension into its calculations. The original relationship of geography and history foundered on the concept of determinism —hardly an astonishing debacle—since both subjects, in their formative stages as academic disciplines, had been looked upon as sciences, with all the philosophical hazards involved in that nineteenth-century attitude. Still worse, the geographers, who considered themselves heirs of Darwin or Lamarck and the evolutionary tradition, saw history as an aspect of environmental or behavioral psychology. This inevitably led them to the arrogant conclusion that history was the product of environment: that is, geography. The effect on human development of such environmental factors as climate had long been discussed, although the central claim and show piece example of geographical determinism had already been dismissed by Hegel with the remark that, where geography had produced Greeks, he now saw only Turks. Early scientific geographers continued to find the determinist position irresistible even after historians had rejected it as logically untenable and psychologically unacceptable.

At the same time, however, historians were having their own difficulties with the problem of determinism. Their predecessors, who had taught by example, had used the concept of causation, not only with no concern for its philosophic consequences, but also without any idea that this well-established moral tradition would conflict with the new scientific history. When they recognized that, in the physical world, respectable causes produced universal, unvarying results, an increasing number of historians found themselves confronting a troublesome dilemma. Either, it seemed to say, history must abandon all causation or it must accept total determination. Even escape via "influence" collapsed under careful scrutiny into "part-time" or "half-hearted" causation. Nor was the embarrassment eased by the fact that determinism had become popularly identified with a notorious analysis of history and an inflammatory doctrine of revolution.

For most historians, determinism was unacceptable on the simple grounds of personal experience; but because they had been drawn to history by some sense of purpose in human affairs, they were unprepared to accept the logical alternative to determinism, which is chaos. Unable to resolve the dilemma, most historical scholars sought refuge in research and the establishment of a verified sequence of events. This may not have provided a logical solution; but it offered a way of life by avoiding the very mention of determinism. And one of the principal threats to this *pis aller* was geography. Its slightest evocation, even in the form of a pictorial setting, tended to imply influence and to break the spell. Under these circumstances, geography was easily sacrificed for historical peace of mind.

In one of the most interesting and persuasive recent attempts to resolve the dilemma of determinism, Professor Arnold J. Toynbee advanced his formula of "challenge and response." This phrase, although it has been widely assimilated into our historical vocabulary—largely as a literary embellishment—was originally conceived as an argument to shift the focus of action, and therefore responsibility, in history from geographic and economic factors back to man, himself. The environment, according to Toynbee, presents man with a situation in which he is free to act in any way he chooses. By eliminating the old problem of the same geographical conditions producing different results at different times, however, he separated man from his environment and therefore from the study of geography. Geographers were not slow to respond to this infringement on their discipline, and Professor O. H. K. Spate charged that "challenge and response" was a mere tautology.

The argument is simple and well known: the environment to which Professor Toynbee would have man react does not exist apart from man himself. In the words of the Committee on Historiography of the Social Science Research Council, which Toynbee cites in discussing Spate's objections to his formula, "No product of nature can be considered a natural resource until Man wants it for his use and has techniques for exploiting it" (*Bulletin* 64, N.Y., 1954, p. 119). From this premise Professor Spate argues that since environment (the totality of natural resources) is a function of human capacities, to separate man from his environment is to divide an indivisible whole, reducing the concept of challenge and response to nonsense. Toynbee grants Spate his logic, but counters with two assertions: first, that all actual knowledge or understanding depends on segmentation of the subject, even if the operation does damage to the totality of reality; and second, that, tautological though it may be, the concept of challenge and response is useful as a myth in the Platonic sense, "to transcend the contradiction between logic and experience" (*Reconsiderations*, Vol. XII, *A Study of History*, Oxford, 1961, p. 253). The wide literary acceptance of Professor Toynbee's formula by the literate public suggests that it does, in fact, correspond to general experience. It also raises the question why it should be necessary to resort to "myth" to circumvent patently misleading logic. In the physical sciences, any logic that controverts a demonstrable proposition is re-examined and usually replaced. If the same procedure were applied to this semantic obstacle, man's relation to his environment could be described in terms that corresponded to general experience, thus re-establishing a useful relationship between history and geography.

If environment exists only in terms of man's needs, desires, and capacities for satisfying them from materials at hand, it accordingly depends on his conscious awareness of his situation. One of the fascinating hypotheses of pre- and early history is that man had to learn to distinguish himself from his surroundings, to recognize the limits of his voluntary control within the circle of his experience. Until he learned to disengage himself from his setting—to distinguish between self and other—he was incapable of conceiving an environment. The ability to focus attention, at will, on different aspects of reality is the basis of consciousness itself. Environment, that is, depends on consciousness, and consciousness depends, not on identity with, but on a clear sense of differentiation between environment and self. Thus there is no tautology in Mr. Toynbee's "challenge and response."

In saying that man alone could transform geography into environment, moreover, the Committee of the Social Science Research Council was obviously not proclaiming the unlimited triumph of mind over matter. It did not say that man could transform any particular segment of geography into the exact environment he wished; and few social scientists would be likely to object to the proposition that the specific environment any given man could create from any given bit of territory would, in practice, impose inherent limits on his potential achievements. The American continents existed geologically, much as we now know them, before the first humans crossed over from the Eurasian mainland. If the Americas only became an environment with that migration, they also became a very different environment with the arrival of Columbus and the Spaniards. But if the New World was a different environment for the Europeans than it had been for the Indians, it was also a different environment for the European invaders than their homelands of Spain or England.

Average men, coordinating their efforts, could, for example, extract significant quantities of gold from only certain special areas, a fact that lent special significance to the environment that Europeans found in the Americas. Conceivably some future descendants, in control of now nonexistent techniques, will be able to produce gold in almost any corner of the earth; but there might still be things they could not do. Even if men, given the state of their technical resources and their interests, do transform geography into environment, geography still limits the kind of environment they create. Man and his environment are neither, at one extreme, identical, nor at the other, independent; but their connections as well as their divisions are difficult to describe.

In these terms, an independent and viable relationship exists between geography and history. The fact that the potentialities as well as the limitations of human action, in any geographic situation, reside in man himself eliminates the false threat of determinism. Men act on, or within, their environment, while geography—in terms of human experience—is inert. Any given men, at any given time, in any given geographical setting, will, in a very practical sense, be limited by the environment; they will, that is, be able to make it respond to their needs or wishes only to the extent of their capacities applied to the objective physical situation.

To identify the geographical factor and trace its role requires a definition of terms. In a widely quoted passage, Professor Carl Sauer defined geography as "what happens in space." Until recently space referred to the surface of the earth, and man's relations to it were usually described in terms of his ability to move across it and extract nourishment, and eventually other resources, from it. Any implication of determinism can be eliminated by formulating the environmental factor in terms of the limitations in man's capacities and in his physical surroundings. An illustration of this sort of limit is the model of a primitive village. Its size depends on the quantity of food that its inhabitants can raise on the available adjacent land, given existing techniques of farming, and within the radius of practical transportation of crops and daily travel to and from work, again, given existing means of transport.

Men's relation to the land they actually farmed, or otherwise exploited, involved an extent of territory and can be described as what geographers call the areal dimension. Villages, however, represented fixed points, and the relations of men in one such location with those in another depended on the distance between them, or the linear dimension. Finally, the natural resources of one limited area or specific location, relative to another, in terms of current human needs and abilities, varied in a third, or qualitative, dimension. These three dimensions establish the context of man's exploitation of the earth.

The historical emergence and development of villages has become the subject of lengthy and even acrimonious debate among anthropologists. For our purposes, however, we can accept the village as existing on the European continent from pre-Roman times and concentrate on the significant characteristics of these early communities—particularly the way in which they realized the inherent logic of their environment, its potential, and its limitations. Early European villages were agricultural units, most of whose members spent most of their lives extracting food from the soil. Communally or individually, on land arranged in strips or plots, the villagers cultivated their crops. The first geographic limitation imposed on this activity was the quality of the soil. But, given any degree of success, villages would sooner or later have to face the problems created by increasing population. As long as uninhabited arable land was readily available, the obvious solution would be to expand the area under cultivation; but such a process would be limited by the distance the villagers could walk to work and bring crops back. The practical areal dimension of the village, that is, would depend on the practical linear distance from the center to the perimeter of the fields. Once this distance had been surpassed, the efficiency of the unit would drop, and, if land were still available, the incentive to establish new villages would increase.

As soon as the expanding population exhausted the possibilities of areal expansion, the society was forced either to limit its population (as has been observed in oases or on islands), to resort to armed conflict with rival villages for control of new land, or to send its excess population to some distant field of expansion. Eventually, however, the more radical alternative of increasing the production of a limited area by the process of increased division of labor and specialization was likely to be attempted. The simplest and most common form of this response was the development of towns to serve as centers for more trade and specialized services than mere villages afforded.

The geographic limits of the town, as of the village, varied; but their basic pattern of social organization was relatively standard. Where the village had served as a base for daily work in the fields, the town provided a center, the market, for a periodic exchange of goods. If the perimeter of the village fields ordinarily did not exceed the distance a farmer could walk to work each day, the market radius of the town did not exceed the distance the villagers could move their produce. And for practical purposes, this established another fundamental geographic limit. In such a simple society, the principal commodities were food, fuel, and building materials. All were bulky and difficult to move; even the more sophisticated products such as crockery, primitive tools, and simple textiles did not lend themselves readily to exchange over large areas. They were neither easy to produce in quantity nor to transport great distances. Accordingly, while the basic unit of the village could be merged into the larger economic organization of the town, the development usually stopped there.

We know, of course, that men, themselves, have often moved at will across distances on the surface of the earth; but this fact only introduces the next basic geographical distinction: that between transport and travel. If overland transport of bulky products has, until the last century or two, been subject to narrow and essentially inflexible limits, men's ability to make their unencumbered way across country has been all but unrestricted by mere distance. This differentiation between travel and transport may well be the historian's most important, as well as most neglected, tool of geographical analysis.

First, it means that the units of economic organization cannot be larger than the radius of practical transport. In a primitive agricultural situation, that radius will not be very large, a few dozen miles at the most, often less. Second, it implies that this economic radius will also describe the extent of general social contact. Few if any of those committed to the task of producing food will have a larger horizon, for most purposes, than the area within which they can exchange goods. As simple farmers, their normal activities will be limited to the radius of the village economy or, conceivably, to the town trading area. Even though human travel is not subject to anything like the natural restrictions on transport, few villagers would have the economic or social freedom to avail themselves of this geographic possibility.

Travel, in spite of its geographical feasibility, was likely to be a social privilege, which suggests still another important distinction. If the division of labor, in at least some minimal form, was inherent in and essential to primitive economic organization, the surplus food it produced created a different form of specialization within the community. Just as the former was economic, the latter was social; in other words, the purpose of the first was to produce an even larger surplus of food, goods, and services and of the second to consume that surplus in the fulfillment of some specialized function. Finally, since the first involved the co-operation of producers, the divisions of their common task might be called vertical and that which separated them from the non-productive consumers, horizontal. Obviously this describes the emergence of an elite which, if it does not "labor," most certainly serves society by a division of function usually religious, judicial, or military.

Two basic facts apparently governed the relations of the upper and lower groups or classes. First, the relationship is reciprocal. The elite functions are at once needed and wanted by the community and imposed upon it. Second, the capacity of an elite to consume surplus products is, for practical purposes, unlimited. In spite of this, the virtually exclusive channeling of leisure to the established elite is not intrinsically unacceptable to the rest of the community. Productive possibilities in all pre-industrial societies are so restricted as to eliminate any practical problem about raising general living standards by the mere distribution of wealth. The only choice would lie between supporting a small elite or none. Anything more than the barest subsistence would be out of the question for the bulk of the population, no matter what the system of distribution. Without the services of an elite, a primitive community would be defenseless before its fears of the supernatural and the threats of its enemies. While it is possible that the religious-magical-medical functions were the first to produce an elite, in early medieval Europe this phenomenon can be more easily examined in its military-administrative-judicial form.

Sooner or later European villagers became involved in warfare: either they required protection from marauders, or they were driven to maraud themselves. If initially fighting had been the responsibility of the younger adult males and not a prerogative of an elite, except for leadership, in time a distinct military caste emerged. So long as the basic military unit remained the village, the forces involved in military actions were normally small, roughly equal and very limited in their range of action. But in almost any form of primitive combat, superior numbers are likely to prevail; and once the forces of two villages combined against a third, they fought at a marked advantage. There was, therefore, an inherent logic that led inexorably to larger and larger military units. Moreover, since military organization involved the movement of men and messages but not necessarily of goods or supplies, it was not subject to the same geographical limitations that prevented the indefinite expansion of economic operations. As campaigns ranged further afield, lasted longer, or involved more expensive or complicated arms, it became increasingly difficult for the entire male population to participate. The differentiation of a military elite was the natural but fateful step. Not only was such a professional fighting group a serious burden for a village society to maintain, it was usually impossible to disband or dismiss. Even when it did not create its own necessity by involving its communities in perpetual war, it normally imposed and maintained its privileged position by force of its own arms.

This development could be viewed as the origin of class distinction, but the apparent corollary that early societies were ordinarily composed of recognizable classes should be approached with caution. The life of these original agricultural communities centered in their villages and tended to follow ancient patterns. Even when peasants lost their fighting function to a military elite, and were thereby reduced to the status of serfs, they initially retained their traditional, self-perpetuating village structures.

Whether the feudal elite should be considered an exploiting class of the same agricultural society is probably, in part at least, a question of vocabulary; but there would be good reason to treat it as a separate social system. For one thing, the villages that comprised the serfs' societies had very different geographic bases than the systems of communication through which the feudal relations of the knights were formed. If the former were restricted and stable, the latter were unstable and vaguely defined. While it would be wrong to suggest that the two had no interests or objectives in common, it would be even more misleading to treat them merely as rival classes within a single social system. The peasant communities, of course, supported the military elite, which in turn protected them, the one out of necessity, the other out of self-interest. But as soon as the functional separation of the two was complete, each became for the other an aspect of the environment.

The military society, once it had emerged, became less interested in its territorial base, except as a source of support, than in its own internal relations. The basic fighting unit was normally the individual soldier or, at most, very small companies of men supported by the existing economic units of manor or village. Because of their personal mobility, warriors were able to organize in loose groups across distances that bore no necessary relation to the geographical limits of the agricultural communities by which they were individually supported. Their organization was essentially linear, linking unit with unit by the circulation of messages and mobilization of men. Thus unhampered by any rigid territorial restrictions, the average military elite had endless potentialities for realignment and expansion. The inherent logic of such development led, through the extension and elaboration of mutual obligations for mutual respect and defense, to what would sooner or later be called a kingdom. The earliest monarchies were apparently constructed from traditional personal relations and seem not in any effective sense to have developed integrated chains of military command. In keeping with this situation, the kings had neither legislative nor administrative prerogatives; they functioned largely as judicial figures to settle disputes arising from vague or conflicting obligations among their followers. The obvious temptation to assume that the title "monarchy" implied the emergence of some embryonic state should be resisted. The members of the military elite who composed this structure were economically independent individuals who fought together for common gain or mutual protection; without one stimulus or the other, their organizations tended to decompose and to regroup in different combinations, with the appearance of each new incentive.

Within this sort of system the authority of leaders was limited by the fact that they could seldom remunerate, or even supply, the majority of their warriors on campaign except at the expense of their common victims. As a result, tribal kings could not enforce discipline among their followers and had to depend instead on their voluntary cooperation. Only gradually did the chieftains modify this frustrating situation by reinforcing their normally loose military command with what would now be called governmental administration. This transformation depended on two factors: first, the conscious determination of the leader to establish effective control over his followers, and second, the development of some device to implement his decision. The solution of this problem was provided by the introduction, or expansion, of the use of money. By reducing the surplus food and commodities on which the military elite subsisted to the dimensions of a message, royal commanders, operating from a distance, could provide or withhold local economic support for their followers if surpluses existed in the right geographical locations, ready to be tapped on the appropriate occasions. In this way the administrative monarchy could realize its potentialities, but only in conjunction with a corresponding evolution of the economic capacities of its agricultural base, which meant, in ordinary circumstances, the development of market towns.

Important as this economic factor is, it should not be allowed to obscure, as it sometimes has, the role of conscious purpose in the development of monarchical authority. It is not necessary here to establish that purpose created money or that money awakened purpose. What is important is to recognize that, together, these decisive departures metamorphosed the traditional society of agricultural villages and their loosely affiliated military elites into historical monarchies. Such emergent military organizations dominate the opening scenes of European history, suggesting that they may in fact have been its creators. If the military monarchies presage the emergence of historical societies, the ancient village society persisted with the new market towns serving as the point of contact between the two. If these larger communities, or their inhabitants, seldom played an active or decisive role in history, they were essential to monarchical development because of their ability to transmute agricultural surpluses into money.

In the earliest, most disorganized phase of medieval society, the serfs of the manor lived in simple agricultural communities. Among themselves, they were capable of nothing beyond the most rudimentary division of labor, but the horizontal division of function set off the lord of the manor as a specialized defender and exploiter of the community. In practice, of course, a single man-at-arms, which was all most manors could support, given the cost of the dominant form of warfare, was not an effective unit of defense. To protect himself and his economic base, it was necessary for him to enter into the whole endless chain of feudal relationships. This system of reciprocal assistance, described in the texts as "rights" and "duties," provided not only a flexible and resilient defense, but an increasingly aggressive offense. Continued military activity inevitably revealed two basic principles: first, that other things being equal, larger units would prevail over smaller; and second, that able commanders could produce the margin of victory. As a result, feudal leaders tended to consolidate their power and gradually transform existing *ad hoc* relationships into hierarchical organizations culminating in the authority of a prince or king.

The story of this development is a central theme of medieval history. The early Capetians, to take the case of France, were hardly distinguishable from their vassals. Only by the patient and purposeful exploitation of the logic of the emerging system were they able to accumulate prestige and resources until, in the middle of the fifteenth century, their descendant, Charles VII, finally succeeded in establishing a professional standing army which freed him from the traditional dependence on semi-independent vassals. Clearly this marked the coming of age of royal administration, and it also dramatized the nature of the transition. The essential element that had been added to the old manorial-feudal society to produce this new self-sufficient monarchy was money.

Because of the flurry of scholarly discussion surrounding the "transition of feudalism to capitalism," it is important to note that the development referred to here does not involve capitalism at all. The transformation of the feudal society of the early middle ages into the administrative monarchies of the early modern period modified but never succeeded in "capitalizing" the agricultural base. Assuming that feudalism was government by barter—that is, a non-monetary arrangement by which services and products were exchanged, both among and between serfs and nobles, according to the needs and possibilities of a simple agricultural society in which the dominant form of fighting was too expensive for all but a small elite to practice—it seems clear that the emergent monarchies of the early middle ages managed to subvert this traditional system by the purposeful reintroduction of money into existing military-governmental relations. Actually the process involved two quite distinct and lengthy phases. In the first, working within the system, the Capetians managed to reduce feudalism to its logical conclusion in the feudal monarchy of the thirteenth century. While it could hardly be maintained that this stage did not involve the increasing use of money, in transmuted services, such changes were regularly rationalized in feudal terms. Even the kings seem to have seen themselves largely as defenders of order, without realizing that in feudalism anarchy was the norm.

Not until the early fourteenth century did a French king move beyond conventional lines in an effort to use new fiscal methods to extend royal authority in a way that threatened to subvert feudal prerogatives. Despite his famous meetings with the Estates, Philip the Fair did not succeed in establishing new institutional relations between crown and towns; but he did lay the pattern for future efforts. From then on the feudal magnates were on the defensive, which explains much of the history of the Hundred Years' War, the ensuing War of the Public Weal, and probably even the Religious Wars of the sixteenth century. All, however, that needs to be noted here is that, despite its growing resources, the monarchy was never able to complete the subjection of feudalism to administrative government. Sooner or later most of the great princes and magnates came to some kind of terms with the crown, and many of the rank-and-file knights served it as mercenary soldiers. A considerable number of the large provincial landholders, however, were neither wholly assimilated to the monarchy nor reduced to total subservience, with the result that they survived as an increasingly anachronistic residue right down to the French Revolution. This persistence of feudal elements in sufficient numbers and strength to force the calling of the Estates General in 1789 should have provided an effective warning against the widely held hypothesis that the monarchy was the logical conclusion of feudalism. In spite of certain superficial resemblances, the two were profoundly different institutions and should never be confused even though they both rested on, and eventually contested for, the agricultural base of rural France.

CHAPTER TWO

The Rise of Trade, Towns, and the Administrative State

———————•———————

MOST HISTORICAL accounts and analyses of the rise of the medieval monarchies relate the process to the much studied concomitant "rise of trade and towns" in western Europe. While the emerging royal bureaucracies obviously drew their fiscal sustenance primarily from towns, the uncritical assumption that these new centers were basically commercial in origin and orientation has not only confused two separate developments but diverted attention from the fact that at least two significantly different societies coexisted in medieval Europe. A glance at a map will show that many of the most famous commercial cities of the period were located between, rather than within, the rising monarchies, thus challenging the assumption that these two new phenomena were part of a single process. Moreover, if the two categories of towns are compared, those that grew up within the monarchies would reveal striking differences from those that did not. Even if all towns are involved in transactions that can be referred to loosely as trade, the character of this activity runs an enormous gamut; and the critical distinction that separates them into two discrete types is the geographical range of their operations. Most towns continued to live economically within their basic agricultural limits; but some participated in, and developed with, the growing commerce in luxuries that brought products from the Orient across Europe and as far north as England and the Baltic. That this was a lucrative business, by the standards of the time, is beyond question, but that its profits financed the new monarchies is less clear—particularly since its principal traffic normally flowed around them. The frequently noted instinct of men to barter and trade has tended to blur the important differences between the purely local exchange of goods and services characteristic of small, essentially self-sufficient communities, such as the manors or even market towns of medieval Europe, and the contemporaneous long-distance commerce in luxuries or the water-borne exchange of staples that had persisted in the Mediterranean for centuries. To sort out the functions and consequences of these two operations, it will be necessary to establish two basic dichotomies: the first, between trade and commerce; and the second, between land and water transport. If the exchange of local products within the usual radius of the market town is arbitrarily classed as trade, even if the quantities, as in the case of grain, might be relatively large, it will be possible to differentiate transactions such as the importation of costly luxury goods from the Near East, no matter how small the bulk, by categorizing them as commerce. In practice this definition depends much more on the distances and values than the quantities involved and thereby leads directly to the distinction between land and water transport.

Water and land, in the form of rivers and seas, or plains and mountains, each provides different possibilities for, and obstacles to, both transport and travel. Until the recent historical past, man could move on land only by foot, on the back of an animal, or in a vehicle drawn by one or more animals. Over water, he had the choice of some form of raft or boat propelled by river current, oars, or wind. By land, travel was relatively simple if food was available along the way; but the transportation of supplies or other possessions in any quantity for any distance was all but prohibitively difficult and costly, even with the use of animals. Merely to move across water, except in the most primitive fashion, involved considerable investment in ships, not to mention the cost of a crew. Once in operation, however, water transport provided a relatively cheap and easy means of moving goods in quantity, thus radically altering the geographical limitations on economic productivity and social organization. The result was a commercial, as distinguished from an agricultural, society.

One of the most famous examples of such a commercial society was already flourishing along the shores, both mainland and island, of the Aegean at the beginning of European history. Thanks to its peculiar setting, moreover, its characteristic social and economic organization is particularly clear, making it an excellent model from which to draw the necessary definitions. Early in their historical development, the inhabitants of the small steep valleys along the shores of Greece, perhaps in response to mounting population pressures, took to their ships in quest of other small and fertile valleys, where they founded new communities. Moving by water, they enjoyed one possibility denied to growing areal societies. Not only could they maintain regular communications with their new colonies, they could almost as easily exchange goods as messages, thus indefinitely extending the range of their economic base along the seacoasts. This virtually unlimited potential for linear extension of water-borne communications correspondingly increased their opportunities for agricultural specialization, in radical contrast with the rigid limits imposed by the difficulties of land transportation between farm villages and market towns. Commercial cities tended to become highly efficient plantation producers, often employing slave labor, and characteristically depended on other such commercial-plantation cities for those necessities that they no longer produced themselves. In consequence, the plantations of the Aegean cities yielded vastly greater agricultural surpluses than normal inland farming communities.

Water communications provided the ancient Greeks with opportunities to increase the division of labor in their handicrafts as well. The expansion of exportable crops led to the development of container industries, that is, vases to export oil or wine, as well as the large-scale importation of consumer goods. Not only such necessities as food, but a wide variety of luxuries —from bronze to madder, and silk to spices—were exchanged, greatly augmenting available surpluses or wealth. As a result of this specialization, the geographical orientation of the towns shifted from the original areal to a new linear dimension. Instead of depending wholly on their immediate agricultural environs for both provisions and markets, they now lived in intimate contact

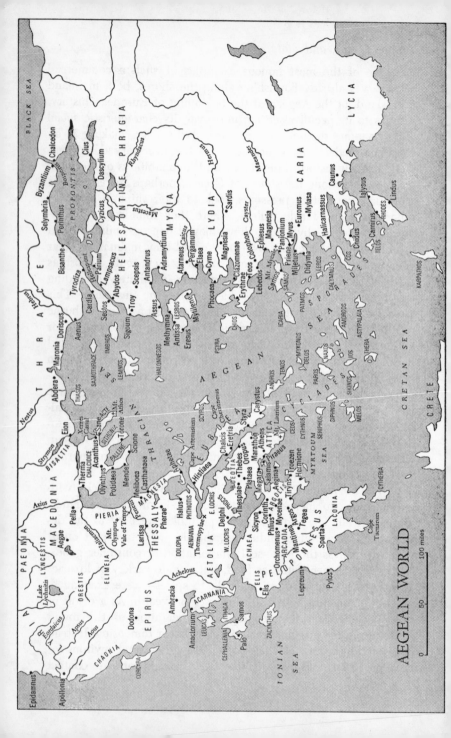

and cooperation with other towns scattered along the littoral of the Aegean. Taken together, these cities formed a commercial society, a system of points through which goods and messages were exchanged.

This development could be carried to two different stages. In the first, the town would tend to feed itself from local sources, exchanging only specialized products; but in the second, it would buy even its food supplies from more or less distant plantation communities. In either case, however, the principal business of the towns would be the exchange of goods in quantity with other commercial towns. It is this that distinguished them from the self-sufficient agricultural market towns and committed them to the interdependence of a large linear (circular) economic system capable of indefinite rationalization and expansion.

This hypothesis of two separate and independent societies, one commercial, the other agricultural, introduces a series of corollaries. First, it assumes that the two models describe the principal types of advanced social-economic organization known to the pre-industrial world. Second, it implies that, although the two systems might make economic contact at random points and even occasionally come into direct conflict, they would tend to operate independently of one another and to maintain their inherent individuality. Next, their different social-economic organizations produced equally distinct governmental-military systems. As a result, each inculcated peculiar interests, attitudes, and reactions—that is, a characteristic social structure—among its own constituent population. What might appear to be the most obvious and significant difference between the two, however—that between rural and urban—can be misleading. If commercial societies were necessarily urban, agricultural communities frequently developed towns and even cities. The critical distinction between the two economic systems lies not between town and country, but between commerce and trade.

Commercial cities, depending on one another for their prosperity, if not survival, normally determined their common interest by consultation and consensus. Even their occasional inter-commercial conflicts did not seriously modify this pattern, perhaps because it was difficult to establish and maintain effective military hegemony overseas. Given this combination of mutual dependence and independence, then, a consultative approach to action proved more practical than constraint and compulsion. Because of this tendency to negotiate, commercial cities have frequently been taken to be democracies when, in fact, they have almost always been ruled by narrow oligarchies. Policies, it is true, were fashioned by agreement, but they usually involved large sums of money, whether for defense, aggression, or investment, and were consequently made by those whose fortunes were involved. Furthermore, the elevation of subsistence techniques to commercial levels of specialization in plantation farming or "factory" manufacture frequently led to the use of slavery.

In contrast, the general organization of agricultural communities has commonly been military, and their government a chain of command. Because security depended on military discipline, obedience was more important than consensus. Where commercial cities were characteristically political, agricultural societies tended to produce administrative institutions. The military hierarchy of officers was paralleled by the administrative hierarchy of civil servants, unless the two functions were compressed into a single bureaucratic system that controlled both state and army. More important than the precise nature of these characteristics within either of the two major types of society, however, is their mutual independence. Even as they evolved into increasingly complex structures, they manifested no tendency to lose their separate identities, at least not until the transportation revolution threatened to destroy and replace them both.

Perhaps the most unfamiliar concept in this analysis is that of geographical dimension. The agricultural society seems familiar because it has territorial or areal extent. The commercial society, by contrast, has generally escaped recognition because it existed primarily in the linear dimension. Having no extended areas to administer, the commercial or linear societies normally had no need for government of the sort we take for granted in the state. Our modern preoccupation with territory makes it difficult for us to think in such terms, and we tend to see the state and society as two aspects of a single reality. Yet, looked at

in a geographical context, the state is simply the normal government of an areal society. Today, for us to recognize the existence
of a society without territory or political administration merely on
the grounds that it maintains itself by an active exchange of
goods and messages, as well as a highly developed sense of common purpose, requires a very special effort.

We know that the ancient Greeks thought of themselves as
constituting a single society, in spite of their inability to achieve
any governmental unity beyond occasional loosely federated
leagues. They were, moreover, wholly persuaded of the fundamental superiority of their city states to the empire of the Persians; and if there is no reason to suppose they attributed their
own special virtues to their environment, the idea that there
may have been some connection between the two has frequently
occurred to later commentators. Imperial-minded British historians
and schoolmasters, for example, read in the conflict between
the Greeks and Persians the lesson that naval training formed
character and fostered democratic instincts while infantry discipline inculcated authoritarian aims and manners. There has
also been considerable debate about the relative military advantages of the two types of society. Each has had its proponents, most notably Admiral A. T. Mahan and his "big navy"
disciples, and Professor Haushofer and the other geopoliticians
with their "heartland" school. Since both doctrines have lost all
practical significance in a missile age, the debate has subsided,
but historically the issue is still important.

Leaving aside the ultimate extremes of sea power attempting
a direct attack on land forces or vice versa, and there are, of
course, famous examples of each, contact between the two must
be made on land, unless the land power has also taken to the
sea. Sea power cannot exist without land bases, while land power
can, and often has, survived without access to the sea. In a
conflict between members of the two systems, the land power
will normally attempt to attack its maritime rival in its cities
and harbors, but if the sea power is based on an invulnerable
island or coast, it will presumably be safe. If, on the contrary,
it is poised on the edge of the land mass dominated by the
military power, it will be seriously exposed. Finally, in a case

such as the Persian War, in which the sea power is based on a distant and difficult shore, the advantages and disadvantages will be so disparate and difficult to assess that either side could nourish hopes of victory. In retrospect, however, that particular war appears to have been an unequal contest, which geography gave Persia little chance of winning. Forced to supply their massive army by sea along an overextended invasion route, the Persians found themselves vulnerable in the Greeks' own element. In the Peloponnesian War, however, the geographic situation was roughly the reverse. Sparta's army, tough though small, was admirably suited in size, training, and the location of its base to the task at hand. In both these cases, it should be noted, the land powers had acquired naval support; and from time to time great powers have attempted to fight on both land and sea. In such clashes, the advantage obviously goes with the dominant land power, if a convenient land frontier exists, or with the preponderant sea power, if contact must be made across water or supply lines must be maintained at sea. Simple as these equations may seem, they need to be stated and remembered.

If the Greeks of the ancient Aegean created the classic model of a commercial society, most of the early empires of the Near East were examples of military-administrative organization of agricultural communities. Rome, however, managed for a time to integrate the two systems into a single governmental-economic operation. A typical agricultural community by origin, Rome became first a small regional capital and then, by conquest, extended its sway over a series of similar capital cities until it ruled the peninsula. Transformed by the Punic Wars into a naval power as well, Rome had managed to conquer virtually the entire Mediterranean littoral by the middle of the first century B.C., thus taking control of the existing commercial society with all its wealth. It was this unprecedented amalgamation of the economic resources of a large and prosperous commercial community with the military potential of a vigorous and expanding agricultural state that provided the base of Rome's incomparable, if not imperishable, power and incidentally laid the foundations of modern Europe.

With the Mediterranean secure, the Roman legions moved

north into Gaul and eventually on to Britain. Whatever the motivation of this conquest, its result was to incorporate western Europe into the *Pax Romana*. Historians have generally assumed this process involved economic as well as military-administrative organization, but if so, it produced an unusual and complicated structure. Rome provided men and money to command the army and govern the provinces. For the comfort and convenience of these officials, goods and luxuries were transported from the Mediterranean to the various imperial outposts, even though they would not have found their way to such remote markets in response to ordinary economic stimuli. Similarly, metals and other provincial products of special interest to the government and army were sent back to Rome from various distant points without normal business concern for costs. In commercial terms, these exchanges were not only artificial, they were limited by the serious difficulties inherent in the overland transportation of such bulky goods. The famous roads, running from hilltop to hilltop, were built for couriers and the exchange of messages, not carts and the exchange of merchandise. If money circulated along these routes, it did so primarily for official imperial, rather than private economic, reasons.

Only one commodity of value was expedited back to Rome in sufficient quantity to integrate the provinces—even partially—into the commercial economy of the Mediterranean: and that was slaves. Not only were slaves a government monopoly in unlimited demand, but they were unusual among natural resources in being self-transporting. Because this lucrative commerce became a critical part of the fiscal-military economy of the Empire does not mean, however, that its administration was rooted in the endless agricultural communities of the provinces, which were affected by the Roman occupation only as it provided them with local markets for their produce. Thus, with the eventual collapse of the imperial superstructure, the indigenous village economies survived to provide a base for successive barbarian regimes until the Franks emerged as the Empire's European heirs.

In a brilliant though much contested thesis, Henri Pirenne has demonstrated that the Carolingians not only turned their backs on the Mediterranean, but also abandoned their Merovingian predecessors' efforts to maintain the old imperial administration. Because it never occurred to Pirenne that able rulers would effect such a change of their own free will, he set out to find the historical factor that had forced their hands. As an economic historian who instinctively understood the role of money in the operation of bueaucratic government, he turned to the Mediterranean commerce in the critical period and found what he took to be his answer in the closing of the eastern Mediterranean to Christian commerce by the Arab conquests of the mid-eighth century. When scholars subsequently demonstrated that Arab control of the eastern Mediterranean was established later and that even then not all commerce ceased, the thesis seemed to be demolished. This criticism, however, merely discredited the causal flourish without touching the far more important insight that the character of the Carolingian regime was a consequence of the Franks' withdrawal from the Mediterranean world. But if Pirenne was mistaken in concluding that they had been driven from the sea, the reason why they "retreated" to northern Europe to create a new power base, which depended far more on personal relationship than money, remains to be established.

Because he found evidence of a lingering trade in luxuries along the littoral, Pirenne assumed that the agricultural society of Gaul was commercially integrated in the economy of the Mediterranean. If, as now seems probable, those economic ties were quantitatively insignificant and the imperial administration of the Merovingians mere vestigial pretensions, then there is no need to seek a Mediterranean explanation of the Carolingian move. The Franks had not been deprived of important revenues by the rise of Islam, simply because the trade from which this income would have had to derive played no significant role in the economy of Gaul. The Carolingians may, therefore, have merely dropped threadbare appearances to concentrate on exploiting important new assets. Whatever was happening to the old fiscal sources, the character of military power was undergoing changes that were, in turn, destined to revolutionize the governmental structure of emergent Europe.

In an undergraduate essay, published in 1885, Sir Charles

Oman demonstrated that heavy cavalry had gradually imposed its sway over the battlefields of Europe, beginning with Adrianople in 378 and continuing a westerly and northerly progress to Hastings in 1066. More recently, Professor Lynn White established that the stirrup, the key to heavy cavalry, was introduced into Gaul just as the Carolingians were preparing to meet the threat of an Islamic invasion from Spain. Perhaps the first of the many far-reaching implications of this innovation was the displacement of money as the lifeblood of the military. The Roman legions, in their time the most sophisticated military organization known, had owed much of their superiority to Rome's administrative, which is to say monetary, base. Being a standing professional infantry, they had to be not only supplied but paid, which was an expense that only such a highly developed fiscal system as the Empire could meet. In contrast, the new heavy cavalry of Charles Martel had different requirements: namely, the provisioning of horses as well as men. Given the bulk quantities this involved, compounded by the difficulties of inland transport, mere money proved irrelevant to a solution of the problem. The only way horses could be maintained was by moving them to the source of supply and distributing them through the innumerable agricultural communities of the countryside.

Thus, no simple lack of funds nor accident of improvisation drove Martel to seize the monastery lands. Not only did these serve as an emergency base for his cavalry, but they provided a model for his and his successors' future policy. As any geographer knows, feeding large animals has always strained the resources of any primitive agricultural economy. Given the limited agricultural capacity of the Mediterranean littoral, it had not been practical to extend the role of horses above their traditional ceremonial function in the ancient world. Charles Martel's cavalry, therefore, depended as much on the development of a new source of provisions as on the introduction of the stirrup. Just at this moment, as Professor White has also revealed, a new, heavy plow capable of handling deep, wet soils, made its appearance in northern Gaul. Although the agricultural and social significance of this innovation has been widely recognized, its military implications have been generally ignored.

The soil of the valleys of the Seine and the Thames, which the new plow liberated, was the deepest and richest of western Europe (even today it grows more wheat per acre than almost any other area in the world). The Carolingians, therefore, suddenly found themselves in possession of two new and complementary assets: the stirrup and the ability to feed an unprecedented number of cavalry mounts. It was a measure of their genius that they sensed and exploited these possibilities by transferring their base of power to the north. Pirenne was probably right in maintaining that the last vestigial remnants of Roman fiscal administration disappeared with the advent of the Carolingians. He was wrong only in attributing this change to an interruption of Mediterranean commerce, instead of to the final withering away of residual and irrelevant bureaucratic institutions.

Resourceful as they were practical, these ambitious usurpers proceeded to organize their own governmental-military system with the most promising elements at hand—a vigorous people and a rich land. Transforming their environment by the use of important technological innovations, the Carolingians effected a military revolution; but powerful as their new heavy cavalry was in action, it could not be maintained as a standing army. Because of the difficulty of concentrating provisions, it had to be disbanded and scattered through the countryside between campaigns. Practical as this arrangement was in terms of logistics and supply, it carried with it the seeds of imperial disintegration. Because the military, and therefore governmental, authority of the Carolingians rested in their cavalry, the dispersion of this force inevitably fragmented their power, which thus took root in smaller and smaller agricultural units. As a result, the basic governmental problem for the next half millennium became the re-establishment of effective royal jurisdiction over endless small, isolated economic-military cells.

In the ninth and tenth centuries, this military system continued to divide and subdivide until its units began to coincide with the basic economic entity of the manor. But just as the process of disintegration approached its ultimate stage, it began to reverse, apparently in response to the stimulus of barbarian depredations. In the northwest, particularly the valley of the Seine, Norse incursions drove the local nobles to replace the moribund Carolingians with a new Capetian dynasty. Probably those responsible never even considered reviving central administration and sought nothing more than a temporary focus for military cooperation within the system of reciprocal defense now known as feudalism. Under the pressure of the invaders, the new leaders were able to exploit these personal arrangements to organize the independent nobles in a loose and unstable, but relatively effective system of mutual protection.

Initially, money could have played no larger a role in the operations of this dynasty than it did in the manorial economies of the nobles; but in the long run, the practice of meeting or avoiding military obligations by monetary contributions became the decisive factor in integrating countless fiefs into medieval monarchies. This gradual revival of a monetary economy and its contribution to the reinstitution of fiscal government is commonly associated with the rise of towns and trade. While there can be no doubt that towns developed remarkably both in number and size and that their economies were the principal source of the new monarchical revenues, the standard interpretation, linking towns and trade, has tended to confuse our understanding of the process.

According to the critical distinction between trade and commerce established above, all towns are more or less concerned with trade in the sense of local exchange and distribution of goods, but only those shipping or receiving goods in bulk, to or from distant points of intensive production or wholesale distribution, are involved in commerce. The traffic in luxuries that developed between the cities of northern Italy and northern Europe originally flowed through the geographic corridor that lies between the Rhône-Seine systems to the west and the Elbe to the east. Within this broad Rhineland path, new towns tended to be commercial, but to either side, their counterparts were seldom more than agricultural market centers. Finally, as any map of the period will show, it was the latter that predominated within the territories of the new feudal monarchies and provided the base on which they were built.

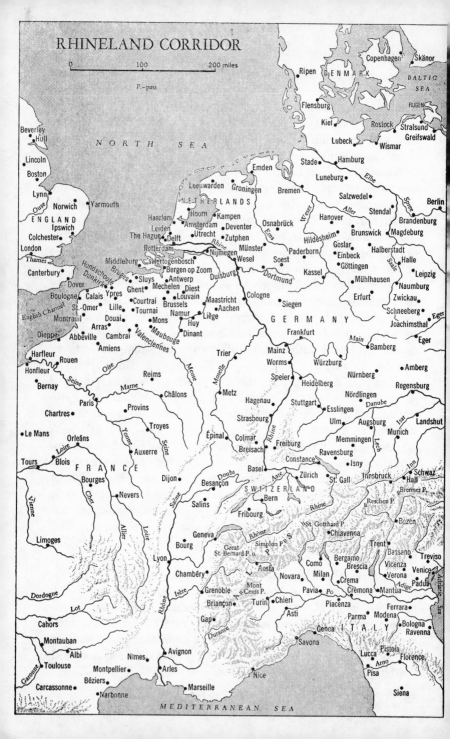

RHINELAND CORRIDOR

0   100   200 miles

P.–pass

In France, for example, towns normally took their place in the organization of the agricultural society by serving either as markets or regional centers for clusters of market towns, feeding themselves by buying from their rural neighbors and providing them with simple manufactures in return. The purpose of this process was to transform local agricultural surpluses into goods, services, and eventually cash, and then to siphon part of this profit off for the benefit of the lord, bishop, or ultimately the king to whom they owed allegiance. To this end, they developed a system of communications through which messages, money, and men moved easily, even if goods could not. Since everything entering towns necessarily passed through fortified gates, the collection of tolls was so obvious and easy a way to tap this wealth that it became a universal practice, giving rise to the modern impression that such dues on trade were in fact tariffs on commerce. Whether or not limited quantities of commercial products occasionally filtered into these market towns, their ordinary source of income was what amounted to mere sales taxes on agricultural supplies coming in from the neighboring countryside.

The new royal towns, therefore, formed the points of contact between local economic units and a countrywide military-governmental structure. Although their economic orientation was territorial, or areal, they also participated in the linear system of royal administration, while the organization of the commercial cities was primarily, if not completely, linear. The agricultural society was a large, expanding administrative-military structure, based on many small and relatively limited economic units, while the commercial community was an extended system of economic relations between governmentally independent urban units. Whereas the former became increasingly concerned with its areal jurisdiction, the latter developed little interest in territory or its political control.

The distinction between the feudal-agricultural and the commercial-urban societies of the early middle ages does not, however, fully resolve the ambiguities created by the hypothesis that the monarchies were fostered by the rise of trade and towns. First, inland towns not only proliferated in this period, that is, eleventh and twelfth centuries, but they tended to serve the monarchical cause and were, in fact, often established by royal charters. The actual function of these towns—in the development of the feudal monarchies and their transformation into national kingdoms—has, however, been confused by the assumption that they were the local agents of a general trade in grain and other agricultural products. That such a commerce flourished along the shores of the English Channel and the Baltic Sea is amply documented, but surprisingly few records have survived to support the thesis that it extended inland.

Although more often taken for granted than discussed, the hypothesis of a general grain trade has been explicitly formulated by such distinguished scholars as Professors M. M. Postan and Georges Duby. Both concede that satisfactory documentation is elusive, but both also warn against underestimating the importance of the trade. Obviously, the circulation of grain fills what would otherwise be a bothersome gap in this widely accepted interpretation, lending it a certain plausibility that is by no means vitiated by the mere absence of substantiating documents. The demonstrable difficulty of overland transport, however, automatically raises such trade to the level of a remarkable achievement and, in turn, makes the lack of documentation more surprising. In such a situation it would seem logical to give the general assumption precedence over the *ad hoc* explanation, at least until more persuasive corroboratory evidence could be discovered.

Facing this sort of problem, historians obviously look for correlative evidence. Professor Postan, for example, has called attention to the rapidly increasing and expanding economic activity of the period, for which there are abundant records, particularly in the areas adjacent to the English Channel, the North Sea, and the Baltic. This undeniable expansion of the economy of northern Europe, however, raises two more questions: first, how far and how regularly its products moved inland except by navigable waterways, and second, whether they constituted trade or commerce as defined in the preceding chapter. In an attempt to resolve objections to his proposition, Professor Postan discusses the means of transportation available for such a trade. He advances the existence of carts and carters, documented by schedules of fees and the occasional records of specific shipments of special goods as reasonable confirmation of his assumption.

To the historical geographer, however, these arguments are not fully persuasive. Aware of the impact of the transportation revolution in the nineteenth century, he knows that in more recent but still preindustrial situations, particularly those that were carefully observed and reported, extensive overland shipment of anything as bulky as grain has proved unreasonably difficult or prohibitively expensive. Even granting that special circumstances produced astonishing exceptions (such as packing wheat across the Andes to feed slaves in the silver mines of Peru) unless confronted with irrefutable evidence of such improbable activity, he will remain unconvinced. His skepticism, moreover, will lead him to seek further tangential documentation.

The specific examples of general trade cited by Professor Duby and others tend to involve either luxuries, wine for a bishop, emergencies, wheat for famine areas, or relatively short hauls to or from water transport, most of which would seem to fall in the category of trade: the distribution of goods to the consumer, normally in small quantities and for important profits. Further, if these transactions reached the quantitative level of commerce, they could be expected to produce concomitant developments that would have left some discernible mark on their society. Modern experience suggests that extensive overland transport should produce traffic problems that could hardly have gone unnoticed and unrecorded. And yet, medieval records contain surprisingly few comments on the existence, conditions, and maintenance of roads, not to mention the volume and routes of traffic. Even without statistical records, it should be possible to estimate the overall volume of the assumed trade in units of cart loads and to project their impact on the all but nonexistent roads and bridges. This kind of quantitative extrapolation has long since been used to deflate overly enthusiastic reports of the size of military forces and might well be applied to current assumptions of preindustrial inland trade. Enough carts to have moved the required quantities, lined up end to end, would surely reach to an absurd conclusion.

But a general trade in grain would have left its mark on more than Europe's roads. Of necessity, it would have reconstituted its entire economic and social structure, transforming its agricultural market towns into commercial cities with all the far-reaching effects that implies. To get the measure of this sort of change, one need only turn back to the ancient Aegean and its classic model of a commercial society. In that maritime world, transport was so easy that the basic division of labor could be extended through the entire commercial system. Far from being self-contained, the cities were units of specialization within a highly sophisticated and unprecedentedly productive community that was based on the export of grain from agricultural plantations to urban centers and the return flow of a variety of specialized commodities in exchange.

These Aegean cities, as has already been noted, characteristically depended on distant grain or olive plantations for their provisions and were thus free to turn their productive energies to the manufacture of vases and textiles or to the building of ships. In the later middle ages, some commercial cities of this sort, living largely on imports, could be found along the shores of the Atlantic and Baltic, where they were beginning to emerge, or on the Mediterranean littoral, where they had continued since antiquity. The recorded difficulty of provisioning inland cities— a problem that became increasingly acute with time—documents the fact that they had no easy access to commercial food supplies. At the same time, grain continued to be raised in all regions of Europe, not just in a few concentrated plantation areas; and most local communities remained essentially self-sufficient neither importing nor exporting significant quantities of food.

The reason so many eminent medievalists cling to the hypothesis of a demonstrably improbable general trade in grain would appear to be that they find it necessary to explain the existence of the general European economy of the later middle ages. Instinctively they looked for the widespread circulation of some basic commodities and found that grain, wine, and a variety of other products were being traded around the Baltic at the time. Even if, as Professor Duby admits, records of grain shipments do appear to stop at the water's edge, they have felt justified in assuming it must have continued inland to account for the general integrated economy they know existed. If, however, the lack of records of any significant internal commerce were taken at face value, then some other hypothesis would be needed to explain the emergence of the general economy.

The one thing that is known to have circulated freely and increasingly, of course, is money, and the dominant agent of the traffic was the monarchy. Is it possible that the developing royal administrations of the later middle ages actually played an economic as well as fiscal and governmental role? If only for lack of an obvious alternative, the idea seems worth consideration. The insatiability of royal appetites for money is legendary, and the uses to which royal treasures were put are legion. The basic objective of most kings in their pursuit of income, however, seems to have been the need to pay royal officials. Centuries of experience had driven home the lesson that only those servitors who were both dependent on, and well supported by, the king could be counted on to remain devoted and effective. As the employment of such bureaucrats proliferated not only at the court but throughout the realm, these "new men" of the king were in practice supported by local surpluses, which they bought with their royal wages. Tax income was dispensed increasingly for local provisions and services, and when the monarchy began to support a standing army, royal expenditures became a major factor in the country's economic life.

Money, in the form of taxes, and a market, in the form of bureaucrats and troops, transformed the production of isolated localities into a general economic system. By circulating the market, in the form of men, and by circulating value, in the form of money, the monarchy became not merely a business nor even the biggest business, but the inclusive business of the realm. The effect of this transformation was, on the one hand, to stimulate the countless local subsistence economies and, on the other, to tie their newly found fortunes to the monarchy. The impact of this relationship can be seen most clearly in the structure and development of urban centers from the smallest towns to Paris. The necessity of paying taxes was an incentive to increase production, and the needs of the army and administration provided both an outlet for surpluses and a source for money income. In other words, the new monarchies created not merely new fiscal-military systems of communications but integrated economies, as well as providing a solid structure within which new areal, that is, national, societies would develop.

Initially, of course, royal bureaucracies were as linear in their organization as the feudal society in which they developed, but by organizing the local agricultural economies around the new market towns, they subverted the old manorial system and began the process of territorial integration. Not merely did the royal administrators struggle to convert the king's vassals into subjects, they also, by implication, undertook the transformation of serfs into peasants. In this new context the appearance of Joan of Arc seems less precocious and astonishing than in the traditional accounts. As the daughter of a peasant, she may well have understood instinctively that the salvation of all peasants depended on the monarchy. If she dreamed of France, it was personified by her King, for whose coronation at Rheims she gave her life; and it was obviously no mere accident that it was he who established the first standing army in French history, thus completing the structure of the monarchical society. It is important to remember, moreover, that despite Joan's passionate hatred of the English, the fulfillment of her mission depended at least as much on the subjection of rebellious French nobles as the expulsion of the "Goddams."

The latter, in fact, was to prove the much easier task, to be completed for all practical purposes by Charles VII himself, while the problem of pacifying the nobles was to occupy, not to say threaten, the monarchy for nearly three more centuries. Only by a desperate struggle was Louis XI, Charles's strange son, able to survive the vicious feudal counterattack known as the War of the Public Weal; and his successors seem to have avoided similar threats only by leading their turbulent vassals on foreign expeditions. Charles VIII, Louis XII, and Francis I all made forays into Italy, and Henry II used the energies of his nobles to defend the boundaries of the realm. Under the last three Valois, France all but disintegrated in the Religious Wars which were fought as much in defense of feudal prerogatives as either "true" faith. Only under the Bourbons were royal authority and public order finally restored.

The moral of this tumultuous story would seem to be that, if Joan had sensed the emergence of a new French nation in the reviving monarchy, this institution and its supporters had had to win a long and desperate struggle to establish the royal France of which she dreamed. It was a civil war fought not between two nations, since all contenders were at least geographically French, but between two societies, each determined to survive in the same country. The fact that the new monarchical state had grown out of the old feudal society did not ease the situation in the least. Even if most of the nobles might have been able to continue coexisting with a feudal monarchy, this new administrative institution, and the monetary economy it engendered, threatened them with extinction. Not only did the monarchy put the subsistence economies of the manors under pressure to produce surpluses that could be turned into tax income through the emerging market towns, but it also began to force its jurisdiction into the hitherto largely independent fiefs. Because of the monarchy's inherent areal character, it left less and less room for the old linear organization; and the incomplete and, therefore, unstable resolution of this conflict arrived at by the Bourbons as the price of power eventually brought the *ancien régime* to its catastrophic conclusion.

CHAPTER THREE

The Origin and Growth
of the
Commercial Community

———————•———————

IF THE RELATIONS between kings and nobles were largely limited to a simple struggle for power, those between the monarchies and the commercial cities were complicated and symbiotic. Not only did the territorial rulers and their courts provide an important part of the ultimate market for the commercial cities, but the wealth produced by commerce was a continuing temptation to chronically impecunious monarchs. In the long run, moreover, the economic and financial exchanges that took place between the two separate systems proved to be quite as important for the development of each as their own internal transactions.

Before examining this relationship, as it developed in the later Middle Ages, it might be useful to recapitulate the history of the two systems as they emerged in post-Roman Europe. For the territorial society, it begins when the Carolingian monarchy abandoned its ties with the old Mediterranean world. Contrary to Pirenne's assumption, the inhabitants of Gaul had not participated directly in the Mediterranean economy during the Roman occupation, so that when the imperial administration finally disappeared, the local agricultural communities were not significantly affected. In spite of the Carolingians' initial military successes, their imperial organization soon revealed organic weaknesses that led to its rapid disintegration. The subsequent history of medieval Europe is often narrated in installments: the first describing anarchy; the second, feudalism; the third, the rise of the feudal monarchies, with the simultaneous growth of towns; and the last, the new monarchical states, whose appearance coincided with the end of the Middle Ages. But if the hypothesis of a general European economy based on trade in such common and bulky commodities as wheat and wine, as well as the famous luxuries, is re-examined in terms of what are posited here as geographical limitations on transport, it seems necessary to reconsider and reformulate a number of standard interpretations.

Even granting that the growing overland commerce, which coursed through the Rhineland Corridor from the Mediterranean to the North Sea and the Baltic, nourished a class of independent towns, there is no need to link them, closely or directly, to either the new market towns or the rising monarchies. Instead, they should be viewed as distinct and largely independent social systems. Even today, any alert observer driving across France and into the lower Rhineland, will be struck by the physical difference between the towns of the two areas. The great guild halls that dominate the commercial cities of the Corridor are seldom found in French provincial towns, which are focused on the cathedral and the market, often covered. The historical record reveals that the governmental and social organization of these different urban units was quite as dissimilar as their physical appearance: one characteristically dominated by an oligarchy, the other by an officer of the crown. In France the bourgeois were the traditional allies of the king in his long struggle with the feudal magnates; in fact, their towns were an integral part of the royal system and prospered with it. But no such attitude toward central authority could have been found among the burghers of the Corridor; instead, they defended themselves vigorously against all territorial encroachments, whether feudal, royal, ecclesiastical, or imperial. Like the cities of the ancient Aegean, their natural form of organization was the league. Sometimes league struggled against rival league for commercial advantage; other times they defended themselves against the territorial amalgamation that was one of the dominant themes of medieval history. In spite of this almost symmetrical dissimilarity, how-

ever, these two emerging societies created the Europe we now
know. It is necessary, therefore, to consider both their separate
development and their contacts, conflicts, and common efforts
in order to understand its history.

The concept of two coterminous societies raises problems of
definition: first, of the phrase "same (or single) geographical
body," and, second, of "society." To be of any interest, this per-
ception must imply something more than mere territorial con-
tiguity, on the one hand, and superficial political divisions within
a single culture, on the other. We are not, that is, in the habit of
thinking of two or more independent social systems cohabiting
the same territory, whether large or small, so that their lines of
communication and exchange would actually interpenetrate. To
some the very idea might well appear a contradiction in terms,
even though careful scrutiny of the map of feudal Europe leads
to the same conclusion.

Since feudal society was, in the terminology established in
the first chapter, linear rather than areal, it did not *occupy*
territory in our contemporary sense. Once this point is recognized, it is obvious that the social structure of medieval commerce was equally linear and that both did exist within the
same geographical body of Europe without drawing boundaries
to define territorial spheres of interest. While the lines of feudal
relationship extended to virtually all parts of the Continent, those
of commerce were generally confined to certain favorable zones,
notably the corridor; but the two were never formally separated
until the emerging national monarchies of the later middle ages
found the corridor cities more difficult to amalgamate into their
territorial states than the traditional fiefs. Needless to say, this
does not mean that the commercial cities had not previously had
to defend themselves against feudal ambitions. Their wealth
made them an all but irresistible temptation to rapacious nobles,
but it also made them virtually invulnerable. The massive
fortifications and mercenary troops that the cities could, and
did, afford turned them into super-castles too strong for ordinary feudal depredations. Even if individual commercial cities
were from time to time brought under feudal, ecclesiastical,
or imperial control, the overall history of the communes of

northern Italy, the Low Countries, and the Free Cities of the Empire suggests that these urban units not only saw their interests in particularistic terms but were prepared and able to defend them. While this does not prove that they constituted a separate and coherent society, it does suggest that they never became integral parts of feudal Europe.

To establish the proposition that the feudal and commercial systems inhabited the same medieval space might seem a Pyrrhic victory, unless it could also be demonstrated that these structures did, in fact, constitute distinguishable, discrete societies. Since they apparently shared, along with the territory, the religion and the languages of Europe, it is reasonable to ask how significant their differences really were. If feudalism, as a system, was nourished by the agricultural production of endless individual manors, it was loosely bound together by the circulation of messages and men in the practice of military protection. The commercial society depended for its existence on the circulation of goods, by water transport where possible, and on messages, in the form of orders and payments. These are really very different operations, and there is a good deal of traditional evidence to indicate that they did not ordinarily mix. The condescension still inherent in the word "bourgeois," the long persistence of the snob value of land, as well as the survival of prejudice against gainful employment among European aristocrats, are random but obvious examples. And certainly nothing would justify representing the burghers of the early medieval cities as the middle class emerging between the serfs and lords.

To describe the boundaries and enumerate the contacts between the two systems would be an enormous undertaking. Unlike the commercial community of the ancient Greeks, the corridor cities were not sharply differentiated from their agricultural neighbors by language and geography. Even so, once their separate existence is suggested, it seems obvious. Like their remote predecessors of the ancient Aegean, the citizens of the commercial communes had special incentives and opportunities to develop intellectual skills and sophistication. Commerce, with its dependence on records and distant communication, put a premium on written records. The exchange of messages, no matter how materialistic, inevitably encourages the exchange and comparison of attitudes and ideas. It has been generally assumed that this sort of experience contributed to the intellectual development of the Greeks; and there appears to be no reason why it might not have had a similar impact on the medieval corridor. Knights, by contrast, were not renowned for literacy and habitually left the care of written records and messages to clerics. Instinctively, they depended far more heavily on memory and tradition, as demonstrated by their literary dependence on the troubadours and the *chansons de geste*. Moreover, if the monastic clergy should be treated as an adjunct of feudal society, their preservation of manuscripts and development of the art of illumination do not represent the same easy familiarity with literacy characteristic of the commercial bourgeoisie.

When, as often happened, one society borrowed a style or institution from the other, it tended to put it to a different use. The early schools of law in northern Italy had no contemporary counterparts in feudal Europe; but a persuasive case can be made for the hypothesis that the great universities that began to appear in the feudal north in the thirteenth century owed not only their origin but their celebrated scholastic method to the example of these Italian prototypes. The feudal monarchs and their ecclesiastical collaborators, however, adapted the model of the legal faculties to their own interests and ends. Not only did they make theology the sovereign subject of their curriculum; but when they studied Roman law, they tended to read *imperium* where their Italian predecessors had found *proprietas*.

Architecture provides another striking case of borrowing, but in reverse. Possibly the most important cultural achievement of feudal Europe was the Gothic. Forced to master masonry in order to build the castles essential to survival, feudal society transmuted a mere craft into a major artistic talent that produced the great cathedrals of northern France and southern England. The rich burghers of the corridor, long in the habit of adapting feudal military architecture to the walls of their cities, also assimilated the Gothic style—not merely for their churches—but characteristically for their great town halls and private palaces. These poles, cathedral and town hall, authority and property, serve as well as any to establish the contrasting orientations of the two systems and when brought into proper focus illustrate the contention that two distinguishable cultures did in fact inhabit the single geographic body of feudal Europe.

Once the existence of recognizably separate societies in medieval Europe is accepted, the possibility arises that some such distinctions may have continued to divide the continent during the transformation of feudal monarchies into nation-states and the vast expansion and redeployment of European commerce with the opening of the Atlantic. Simultaneously with the emergence of national administrative monarchies, notably in England, France, and Spain, Europe's commerce broke out of the Mediterranean-corridor–Baltic pattern in which it had been formed. The famous incident in which Queen Isabella celebrated the completion of the *reconquista* by supporting Columbus' first voyage might even suggest that the monarchs themselves contributed to this reorientation; actually the change was already well under way in ·1492. Not even the traditional attribution of the move into the Atlantic to the consolidation of Turkish power in the eastern Mediterranean in the middle of the century stands close scrutiny. As Europe's general economy had expanded, its market for luxuries had increased. To meet this new demand, Italian merchants had opened the famous Atlantic galley service from the Mediterranean to the North Sea and the Baltic, thereby increasing the volume far beyond that previously carried over the old pack routes across the Alps, but also far in excess of the quantities that the caravan routes through the Near East could supply. There are clear indications that the idea of an all-water route, capable of meeting this new quantitative dimension, was considered as early as the thirteenth century; and by the early fifteenth, the Portuguese had inaugurated their program of exploration. Thus, by the time their campaign to sail around Africa was making important progress, the idea of reaching the sources of oriental commerce by water was hardly new.

If, however, no causal relation, in either direction, between the development of the new monarchies and the Atlantic commerce can be established, the two do become involved in an important, if symbiotic, relationship by the early sixteenth cen-

tury. The fundamental purpose of both the commercial community and the monarchical administration was to generate surplus wealth in the form of money. If commercial economies
tended to produce greater profits than they could normally consume in goods or absorb in reinvestment, agricultural kingdoms
required more capital investment than they could themselves
provide. Unlike their feudal predecessors, the new administrative
monarchies could and did collect regular tax income from the
agricultural society of Europe, but they needed ever more cash
to maintain and expand their administrative organizations. If,
therefore, the monarchs of the sixteenth century could continue
to develop their royal ventures only by borrowing, their burgeon-
ing state machinery did produce enough revenue to guarantee
and service an expanding debt. It was hardly surprising that this
opportunity should have been discovered and exploited by the
commercial capitalists of the time.

According to the hypothesis advanced some years ago by
Professor Robert Lopez, the Italian Renaissance was partly the
product of a depression that curtailed the customary possibilities for the reinvestment of commercial profits. For lack of other
opportunities, he argued, Florentine bankers began to place their
funds in art. Whether or not Professor Lopez overrated the
severity of the depression, as his critics now contend, he does
call attention to the important fact that the Medici and their
rivals were investing heavily in culture. Whether the cause was
a business depression seems to be far less significant than the
evidence this outlay offers that there was more capital available
than could be absorbed in normal commercial enterprise. The
same pressure of profits might easily appear to account, at least
in part, for funding the first royal debt in France early in the
sixteenth century. The vigor of the French monarchy had been
rudely called to the attention of the Italians by a series of in-
vasions of their peninsula; the development of their interest in,
and contribution to, that institution is recorded by the appearance of two Medici queens on its throne and the presence
of countless Italian advisers, administrators, and followers at
the court and in the royal service.

This relationship between commercial bankers and ter-

ritorial princes was to become as basic to early modern Europe
as it might appear unnatural. Founded on the simple fact that
one had a chronic surplus and the other an equally chronic need
for capital, this cooperative alliance was inevitable and irreplace-
able. But it should not be taken as anything more than an *affaire
de convenance*. Utterly unlike the bourgeois of the market towns,
the great merchant bankers were not supporting an institution
to which they owed allegiance; instead, they were availing themselves of a nearly unique opportunity to invest capital where it
could earn interest. As the Atlantic commerce gained momentum
in the eighteenth century, its animators dumped their rapidly
accelerating profits into the only contemporary concerns capable
of absorbing an unlimited amount of credit: the insatiable but
ill-managed royal treasuries, particularly that of France.

In the sixteenth and seventeenth centuries the royal debt had
not yet become a dominant factor in the administration of the
realm. Increasingly, monarchical bureaucrats sought to exploit
the unprecedented wealth produced by the slave trade and New
World plantations through the techniques they had learned in
administering an agricultural kingdom. In an effort to assimilate
commerce to the state, they developed a complex of new policies
that collectively came to be known as "mercantilism," and fostered the widely held misapprehension that the early national
monarchies were essentially commercial. The fact is, the royal
bureaucracies never succeeded in becoming commercial agents;
and their great port cities suffered their interference and exploitation only under duress. Behind this mercantilist façade of royal
controls, the ports seem to have developed into a self-contained
commercial society, economically uniting the shores of Europe
and North America.

Earlier examples of commercial communities—such as the
ancient Aegean, or the medieval Mediterranean, Corridor, and
Baltic—all suggest of course that commerce, in the sense defined
above, tends to create its own society. It need not, therefore,
appear impossible that Atlantic commerce also developed a discrete social structure independent of, and radically different from,
the great administrative states. Indeed, the striking similarities
among the great Atlantic ports of the period have long been

noted and accepted. Studies have been written to show that some, at least, had astonishingly little contact with their immediate hinterland; but the obsession with territorial administration, engendered by the new monarchies, has obscured this critical distinction. To move directly to a pivotal case, was Bordeaux Atlantic or French?

A glance at that city's history would immediately reveal that this was indeed a major issue. Distrustful of and distrusted by the monarchy, since it had been reacquired by Charles VII at the end of the Hundred Years' War, Bordeaux had repeatedly been invested by royal troops, twice in the seventeenth century. Following the second of these latter occupations, a permanent garrison was installed and the *Château de la trompette* rebuilt to serve as a base and symbol of monarchical authority, to be called to the attention of the endemically recalcitrant Bordelais each noon by the blast of a trumpet from its tower. While these details of local history hardly establish a general case, they leave open the possibility that Bordeaux's allegiance to the monarchy was less than total.

A comparison of this seventeenth-century situation with the Aegean model examined above suggests that the Atlantic commerce could have been expected to develop its own integrated economic society and that it would have needed to defend itself against the territorial states that controlled the hinterland. Few of the Atlantic ports enjoyed the geographical protection afforded by the mountains of the Greek peninsula. At the same time, the size of the ocean precluded the possibility of a single power dominating the entire littoral, as Rome had that of the Mediterranean. This raises the possibility that each city would succumb to, and be absorbed by, its own particular monarchy, thereby fragmenting the commercial society, perhaps before it even came into effective existence, and transferring both its focus and its wealth from the ocean, as Adam Smith phrased it, to the nations. If, however, the so-called political history of the age would seem to justify this hypothesis, its economic patterns would not.

Bordeaux, for example, continued throughout the *ancien régime* to draw not only its profits but most of its sustenance from the sea, selling African slaves in the Antilles, importing sugar to

Europe, exporting brandies from its own vineyard "plantations" on the neighboring banks of the Gironde to the Low Countries, and buying wheat and timber in the Baltic. Little of this commerce involved the hinterland of France, except indirectly in the taxes the city paid the crown. The next question to be resolved, therefore, is whether or not this fiscal-administrative relationship assimilated the port into the agricultural areal society of the monarchy, or whether Bordeaux, "occupied" though it was, continued to live in an Atlantic context. And the same question would need to be asked, with appropriate modifications, for all the other Atlantic ports.

It can hardly be mere coincidence that Admiral Mahan found his classic examples of sea power in the history of the seventeenth and eighteenth centuries. Most major military confrontations spilled over into the ocean, even if they began on land and were frequently carried to the ends of the colonial world, as Macaulay so vividly recounted. Historians have long sensed, in the kaleidoscopic events of this mounting imperial struggle, a vast re-enactment of the sea-land confrontations of the Greeks and Persians. In the dramatic confusion, however, the lines of social structure were lost from view.

Between 1640 and 1688, established monarchical authority around Europe was challenged by a number of open insurrections described by Roger B. Merriman as the "six contemporaneous revolutions." Three of these revolts were against the king of Spain; those in Barcelona and Naples failed; that in Lisbon succeeded. All three, it should be noted, broke out in great port cities subject to the authority of a royal, but territorial, administration. In France, the *Fronde* proper was a struggle between the king and his near relatives, the princes, over the distribution of the royal revenues. In the resulting confusion the Bordelais made another effort to assert some degree of independence; this too failed. In the Netherlands, however, the merchant-oligarchs of Amsterdam were able to replace the monarchical stadtholder with their own candidate, who ruled as "pensionary," through the estates, for the next twenty-two years.

Looked at from this perspective, the famous events in England take on an unfamiliar aspect. The Civil War becomes not merely a struggle between ship-owning Whig merchants and the territorial-military administration of the king, but the forceful seizure of a safe land base by the English members of the Atlantic community, at just the time their Dutch and Portuguese colleagues were establishing their own *pieds-à-terre* in the Low Countries and on the Peninsula. These moves, it is interesting to note, were followed by the Anglo-Portuguese alliance, later reinforced by the royal marriage of Charles II and Catherine of Braganza, and a series of cooperative arrangements with the Dutch, culminating in the Glorious Revolution and the installation of William and Mary on the English throne. It was this gradual reorientation that set the stage and drew the lines for the great Anglo-French wars: first, those that defended the Netherlands base of the Atlantic society from Louis XIV; and then, the eighteenth-century struggle between the two for overseas empire as well as the hegemony of Europe.

At the beginning of the seventeenth century, when the Atlantic community was first taking shape, the territorial monarchies that ruled the principal maritime cities viewed them as a most welcome source of income. Not understanding the nature of the new system, however, the monarchs attempted to control and exploit the developing ocean commerce, as they did the trade of their market towns. This not only hampered the operations of the merchants but provoked their opposition and, eventually, rebellion. In this early phase, rival monarchies became involved in trade wars in efforts to corner markets and, as they hoped, to increase their profits. This naked mercantilism failed because its royal practitioners did not realize—as Adam Smith was to point out later—that greater wealth could be realized by increasing rather than monopolizing trade. Because the port cities exchanged goods primarily with each other, and very little with their agricultural hinterlands, any restrictions on their freedom of movement at sea immediately limited their economic potential.

Even following the seventeenth-century revolutions, full realization of the essential nature of commerce spread slowly, and armed conflict over markets continued. With the eighteenth century, however, European wars took on a different orientation, increasingly pitting maritime against continental powers. This struggle reached its climax at the beginning of the nineteenth century, with England's complete control of the seas and ocean commerce and Napoleon's domination of the Continent, which—as Eli Heckscher demonstrated, in his *Continental System*—was as much a plan to rationalize the agricultural economy of Europe as to inflict commercial losses on England. Napoleon's obvious conviction that England, unlike his Empire, could not survive without ocean trade was not entirely mistaken; but the corollary that Europe could survive in such a fashion proved dangerously false. Europe's vast agricultural economy, as he knew, was still largely composed of more or less self-sufficient subsistence units. What he failed to recognize was the size and importance of the coastal population and its dependence on access to the sea, not merely for profits, but even for essential provisions.

One tentative conclusion that can be drawn from a review of seventeenth- and eighteenth-century history, however, is that, while port cities were quite capable of resorting to arms against rivals in defense of their commercial interests, just as fellow monarchs fought one another for territorial aggrandizement, these conflicts tended to be limited, in exactly the sense so often applied to the warfare of the period; because the antagonists seemed to realize that they both, or all, stood to lose if victory seriously damaged the system in which they lived. In confrontations between the two systems, no such limits were observed.

From this majestic panorama, however, it is necessary to turn back to the French ports and ask what we are looking for—what difference, in short, we would expect to find between a commercial or monarchical Bordeaux. This can best be answered by a review of qualities already identified in other commercial and monarchical societies. Commerce, it has already been noted, depends on written records and instructions, which require literacy; involves travel, which invites observation, discussion, and comparison; and deals with other independent and frequently distant merchants, which encourages negotiation and compromise. It is surely no accident that the Venetians established the first modern diplomatic service. Together, these characteristics suggest the urbane, tolerant, skeptical, and pragmatic attitude frequently associated with Georgian England. In their government, commercial societies tend to be political rather than administrative; that is, they depend on some institutionalized form of negotiation and compromise both at home and abroad. If power is reserved for the merchant class, their policies are normally reached by discussion rather than fiat. In the eighteenth century, these tendencies were beginning to manifest themselves in the parliamentary government of England, which had already become the classic model for modern commercial societies. Social and economic patterns would stress the family, industrious habits, and class distinctions, and would be frequently based on slavery. Whether this society produced its own culture or religion is a question too large to settle here, but there are many signs suggesting that particular cultural and even religious styles flourished in the commercial cities.

The territorial-administrative society of eighteenth-century France did not, however, provide the same contrast to this set of values that feudalism had to the commercial civilization of the corridor. For one thing, the royal bureaucracy made increasing demands on literacy; but whereas the *commerçants* turned instinctively to negotiation and compromise, the administrators resorted to decrees and, if need be, judicial arbitration. The monarchy was still essentially a military organization operating through a central chain of command. If the king was not an oriental despot and if he was subject, at least in theory, to constitutional checks, he certainly knew no equals at his court. The elite of the realm was composed of courtiers, not citizens, and society was far more hierarchical than that of any commercial city. Paradoxically, however, and contrary to Anglo-Saxon prejudice, an administrative monarchy might have a "democratic" base.

In a simple agricultural society, the royal army would normally be made up of peasant soldiers. The fact that the cost of weapons in the early middle ages had reduced the peasants to serfs left an unfortunate legacy for the kings of France, who in no sense shared the nobles' vested interest in the perpetuation of servitude. On the contrary, royal agents could expect to collect more taxes and secure more effective military service, from healthy, prosperous peasants than from downtrodden serfs. For this reason the great intendants all established reputations as liberal reformers, and the *philosophes* and other "revolutionary" critics and theorists were read and admired by members of the court. A rational society, not a more manageable government, was their objective; and this, it was widely assumed, could be effected only by a vigorous royal administration.

This particular character of French political attitudes during the *ancien régime* has, however, frequently been missed by historians who assumed that a "democratic revolution" would necessarily aim at popular participation in the governance of the country. Because the French Revolution was precipitated by a constitutional crisis; opened with a pledge to provide the country with a new constitution; and—during its first phase—involved sustained efforts to constitute, and operate, a constitutional monarchy, the impression has been deeply implanted in most accounts of the period that the French were committed to the concept of constitutional government by implication in the form of a parliamentary monarchy. But at the risk of anticipating here and repeating below, it is essential to point out that this is a seriously misleading impression. For most revolutionaries, in 1789 and after, the urgent problem was to make the monarchy work, not how it worked; what they really wanted was to reform the King, not the monarchy. As a result, they were to leave the task of constitution writing—at least until they began to sense its implications—to a comparative handful of interested and qualified deputies.

That these unusual individuals tended to come from port cities, or to have other contacts with merchant or banking interests, was eventually recognized in the label of "Girondins" which they subsequently acquired. To return to the *ancien régime*, it is important to realize that the commercial community did not produce publicists for constitutional reform. Actually its members showed little interest in the mechanics of the monarchy, so long as it paid the interest on their loans and left them alone in other respects. Clearly to them, that government was best that governed least, as they were to demonstrate by aiding and abetting the dissolution of the monarchical administration during the early months of the Revolution.

But if two or more social structures, each complete with its own ethos, did, in fact, exist in France, why have the political divisions they created never been formulated in explicit terms? The basic reason is, of course, that a social structure of the sort under discussion here is relatively discrete and self-contained. The merchants of the ports normally communicated with other merchants in other ports, not with the inhabitants of the interior of France. The royal administrators, because of their territorial obsession, and because of the obvious wealth to be tapped, were determined to bring the ports under their jurisdiction, but this does not mean that they understood them in the slightest. They must have found the resistance of the merchants trying, but it probably never occurred to them that they were dealing with a totally different, foreign, social system.

A state without a visible, organized territorial base would, in their terms, have constituted a flat contradiction. Nor would the merchants have consciously thought of themselves as citizens of an Atlantic state. Instead, there is some evidence that they were by no means persuaded of the necessity of belonging to any administrative state at all. Their own ocean community functioned to their satisfaction, without benefit of bureaucratic apparatus. Thus, by definition, the paths of the respective members of these two societies tended not to cross, except as the monarchy attempted to control, and thereby curtail, the cities' commercial activities. In practice, this meant that the two were scarcely visible to one another. The everyday variety of what are usually called "political differences" did not ordinarily arise between the systems, but rather between the members of each. The political opponent of the royal administrator was a recalcitrant landowner or rival bureaucrat; and of the merchant, it was another commercial bourgeois or perhaps his workers. This made chance confrontations of representatives of the two different systems perplexing and dangerous, because neither really recognized the other's true existence. As a result, they found communication, even using the same vocabulary and grammar, next to impossible. Before considering their relationship and its implications further, however, it would be instructive to examine the body politic of France for signs of other independent social structures.

The peasantry might easily seem the first identifiable segment of the population to consider. Certainly, it was effectively cut off from the upper classes in social terms (exchange of wives and general mobility), but it would be hard to get around the fact that, as the cartoons of the late eighteenth century insisted, the peasants formed the base that bore the monarchy. First, they produced the agricultural wealth on which it lived; and second, they produced the soldiers who filled the ranks of its armies. Moreover, as the Revolution approached, royal ministers attempted to regularize the peasants' fiscal obligations; and finally in the Revolutionary period, the peasants rallied to the central bureaucracy. Once it is established that the peasantry had become part of the monarchical structure, it is not difficult to see that the common opponents of both king and peasants were the great nobles and clerics.

A substantial number of the members of the First and Second Estates was obviously still trying to live in terms of the old feudal structure that had lost its functional justification at least two centuries before. The persistence of a group beyond the disintegration of the social structure in which it had been formed is a strange but not unique phenomenon; and in this case the residue is not hard to identify or describe. Characteristically it was composed of the larger landholders, but not the princes of the realm nor even the constant residents at Versailles. The latter had obviously, if not necessarily willingly, cast their lot with the king. Similarly, many of the lesser nobles had, whether from ambition or necessity, taken service in the army or, occasionally, in the administration. The remaining survivors of the old feudal classes, however, tended to live on their properties in the provinces, serve and subvert the local bureaucracy, seek preferment in the church, and find expression and defense of their interests through the provincial estates and *parlements*. They were, in short, social parasites who, though they lived well, contributed little if anything to their society; and they were looked upon as such not only by the intellectuals, but also by the royal administrators of the day. In fact, the real object of the various reform projects proposed by Turgot and the other great officers of the crown was the reduction or elimination of noble privileges, which in effect meant the liquidation of the nobles as an order.

Some such confrontation was inevitable. Not only was it the

logical conclusion of the struggle initiated by the restoration of
the monarchy in the tenth century, it was the only practical
road toward fiscal salvation left open to the crown at the end of
the eighteenth century. Because the king's principal source of income was the taxes raised on peasant land, the rents extracted
by the nobles from the same overburdened victims constituted a
limitation on royal exactions. This injury was compounded by the
insult of the aristocratic privilege that exempted the nobles from
the basic direct taxes. Any intelligent intendant realized that
the only way to save the monarchy was to end this anachronistic
privilege and to rationalize the obligations of the peasants just as
the nobles recognized that any such reforms meant their own
bankruptcy. In response to this threat, they mounted the best
rear-guard efforts they could, using both the *parlements* and their
influence at court. Poor Louis XVI has been blamed for allowing
them to frustrate his ministers and precipitate the *déluge*, but he
probably had little choice. They were much too large and vigorous a constituency to be liquidated without a struggle.

Because the royal administration, in its formative period, had
not been strong enough to reduce the members of this anachronistic caste to a single service status, it had tacitly offered a compromise settlement by which the nobles' traditional privileges,
notably exemption from any but customary fiscal exactions and
defense of the established rents from their "fiefs," were confirmed by an understanding its spokesmen were later to insist on
calling the "constitution." This phenomenon is of special interest
for two reasons. First, it demonstrates that institutions that have
lost their structural function can still persist more or less indefinitely and second, that their beneficiaries will hold to their
anachronistic attitudes and prejudices with extraordinary te-
nacity.

If this investigation has established the validity, or at least
utility, of the geographic dimension as an analytic tool, it has
also suggested a new picture of modern Europe. In addition to
demonstrating that the mature and dominant monarchical society
shared the geographical body of France with the moribund resi-
dues of the old feudal system, it revealed the existence of an
essentially independent and self-contained Atlantic commercial
economy, that maintained land bases in the country's ports.

To test not merely that hypothesis, but also the analytic techniques by which it was reached, requires that they be applied to the close scrutiny of some limited field of history. For this essay the obvious subject is the political and social development of France since the end of the *ancien régime*. This narrowing of the focus and slowing of the pace of our investigation is not meant to suggest that the methods and concepts developed above are applicable only to modern France but rather to demonstrate that they can unravel as tangled a story as French political development.

CHAPTER FOUR

Contemporaneous Social
Analysis of the *Ancien Régime*

———•———

IF TWO OR MORE discrete and identifiable societies have, in fact, inhabited the continent of Europe at least since the beginning of the middle ages, it is inconceivable that so important a phenomenon should have gone entirely unnoticed until today. The presumption that social analysts of any age could know their own world so little as to miss such a striking feature of daily life would be preposterous; and yet this essay presents it as a "new" hypothesis. That it may be "new" to twentieth-century historians or social scientists does not, however, mean that it would have been unfamiliar to contemporaneous critics—for example, of the *ancien régime* in France. To them it might well have been too obvious to invite much comment, or it might have been described and discussed in terms that subsequently have acquired new, and in this case, misleading meanings. It is the purpose of this chapter to re-examine key works of selected social and political critics of the *ancien régime* in the context of their lives and times in search of evidence indicating their awareness of coexisting societies in the realm of France.

The first modern political theorist in France is generally agreed to have been Jean Bodin. Sometimes credited with having reintroduced the concept of the state into political discussion, he is more widely and justly admired for his definition and defense of sovereignty in a doctrine that has been celebrated for its reconciliation of effective government with constitutional limitations. If his writings are so scholastic in form and style as to make heavy going for modern readers, they contain fresh and

penetrating insights, and a new and revolutionary solution for
the anarchy that was consuming France in the second half of the
sixteenth century. The author's prescription, moreover, was not
only acute, but prophetic, because both the Bourbons and the
large majority of their subjects were to accept, whether consciously or not, his concept of sovereignty as the practical model
of, as well as the theoretical justification for, the restoration of
peace and order.

Born in 1529 or 1530, Bodin began his life in the peace and
prosperity made possible by the unlimited authority of the Renaissance monarchy; but well before his death in 1596, this
tightly reined order gave way to the tumult of the Religious Wars.
Whether or not Bodin was attracted to Calvinism—and the evidence is inconclusive—there is no question that his overwhelming
commitment was to the suppression of religious persecution and
political disorder. To avoid falling victim to the former, he
concealed his own religious convictions; and to do what he
could to reduce the latter, he served the party of the *Politiques*
as a publicist in their campaign to restore civil authority. It
was in this cause that he formulated his famous doctrine of
sovereignty, which would clearly seem intended to re-establish
the political stability he had known in his youth by resurrecting
the monarchy that had maintained it. While he admitted that
such unrestrained power could lead to tyranny, the prospect of
unrestrained chaos drove him to grant, however reluctantly, the
right of sovereignty even to a tyrant. His argument was an
exercise in logic, but his conviction was obviously the product
of experience. For Bodin, even tyranny was preferable to unmitigated civil war.

The hallmark of Bodin's sovereignty was its indivisible and
unlimited authority within prescribed limits. The authority of
the sovereign was absolute in the formulation, enforcement, and
ultimately the interpretation and dispensation of the law. It con-
sisted of the right to make war and peace and to police the
realm; it did not, however, include the right to dispose of the
property of any subject, except in a national emergency and even
then in strict accordance with established procedure. What this
distinction meant in practice was that the nobles would sur-

render their residual rights of government to the crown, on the understanding that their property would not be subject to fiscal or administrative exaction. It becomes apparent, therefore, that the paradox in the limits Bodin set to the ruler's absolute sovereignty is resolved by geographical delimitation. The sovereign's authority was unlimited in the realm at large, but did not penetrate the private preserves of his subjects. Even if this explanation helps elucidate one ambiguity in Bodin's theory, it uncovers another: namely, the nature of the state that he appears to be trying to restore to political discussion. Was it the total entity within which his sovereign was to exercise his circumscribed but absolute authority or was it the institutional agent of that legal power? Merely to say it was the French monarchy helps little unless we can define its extent and explain its nature. What we do know is that Bodin wrote to save France from disintegration.

The only hope of averting this disaster, he believed, lay in subjecting the nobles to the royal administration in all public matters. He also understood that the only possibility of having the monarchical state accepted by these powerful and reluctant subjects depended on the sovereign's recognition of their right to enjoy their property freely and fully. It is significant that Bodin's original Latin term for his new state was *res publica,* the real sense of which can be rendered by neither the French *république* nor the English "republic." The central distinction implicit in this term and in his constitutional solution was the absolute separation of public and private business. Translated into modern terms and concepts, however, this means that the sovereign was only one of two or more powers within France. The king could not be challenged in his realm, but that clearly did not include the totality of France. The state that Bodin helped revive was the first and the most important, but not the only, power within the country.

Bodin seems clearly to have seized on the new administrative monarchy as the one viable alternative to feudal chaos. Even so, to him the state was not, as it is to us in the second half of the twentieth century, the overwhelming fact of social life; therefore, to formulate its nature was an act of creative

imagination. In the seventeenth century, a bewildering variety
of states made a spectacular bid for the preponderant position
they were eventually to achieve in Europe's affairs. As a result,
they were much discussed, but not as the unique, omnipotent,
and monolithic phenomena they have since become. The existence of other socio-governmental organisms was too obvious a
fact of life to call for insistent, explicit mention, particularly
since the commentators of that day did not anticipate our
twentieth-century assumptions. Thus, at least by implication,
Bodin seems to have recognized the existence of two political
systems contending for position and survival in the territorial
body of France.

   To find another, though very different, witness of this same
fundamental proposition, it is necessary to turn no further than
to the Comte Henri de Boulainvilliers. Long celebrated as an
important precursor of the *philosophes,* he is best known for
two works: one on the state of France as revealed by the reports
of the royal intendants of Louis XIV, and a second—in the form
of a memoir to the regent, the Duc d'Orléans—suggesting ways
of increasing the prosperity of the realm. In other philosophical
writings Boulainvilliers commented on Spinoza and expressed a
preference for the religion of Islam. Daring as these last two
intellectual excursions might appear, they actually developed
the most fashionable contemporary views of the church and
caused their author no trouble. His *Essai sur la noblesse de
France,* however, did cause a scandal and, despite the fact that
it was mentioned with approbation by Montesquieu, it continues
to compromise his reputation, which is important because it
tends to divert our attention from the basic argument of this
work. Written in defense of aristocratic privilege, the essay
proposed that the nobility derived its position from the conquest by its progenitors, the Franks, of the decadent Romans and
inferior Gauls. This embarrassing thesis was promptly discredited as historically untenable because its author failed to
establish the direct lineal descent of the contemporary nobles
from the original Franks.

   Although Boulainvilliers' historical evidence was tenuous,
this weakness would hardly account for the displeasure of his

critics. His defense of the nobles' position seems, in some way, to have touched particularly sensitive prejudices. The rights of conquest and inheritance were both recognized by the most respectable legal authorities of the Enlightenment, and privilege was taken for granted. His resort to history, however, may well have affronted the sensibilities of the eighteenth century by appealing to the past; even more than the obscurantism of the church, the *philosophes* resented the dead hand of tradition. The only history they really valued was that which they saw themselves enacting; and the only justification for society that they were prepared to accept was one that followed what they took to be reason. Given this attitude, which Boulainvilliers must surely have sensed, why did he deliberately flout the established canons and risk the quasi-excommunication he suffered?

He may, quite simply, have felt a need to defend his fellow nobles. In the emerging rationale of the administrative monarchy, the position of the nobility was being treated as an anomaly. But from his own experience, Boulainvilliers knew that this ancient order still existed and had been neither totally subdued by, nor wholly assimilated to, the monarchy. If he had enjoyed access to twentieth-century terminology, he might well have called them a "class"; but from his own vocabulary, the word he chose was "race." The nobles were, after all, inheritors of privileges, originally based on, or derived from military power. Why not then defend their position in terms of an inherited right of conquest? Today we might wince at his unblushing appeal to right by conquest, but we might also be less concerned about the actual genealogical descent of the eighteenth-century nobility from Charlemagne's mounted warriors, because we would recognize in them the historical founders of a self-contained, though anachronistic, social order. And even if we refused to accept Boulainvilliers' defense of hereditary privilege on any grounds, we would have no trouble understanding its transmission from generation to generation by a self-perpetuating elite whether or not it constituted a biological "race." It is clear, therefore, however we react to his argument, there is evidence Boulainvilliers recognized the existence of one of the additional societies we have attempted to identify in early modern France.

In a canvass of contemporaneous criticism or analysis of the *ancien régime*, the most important text is unquestionably the *Esprit des Lois* of Charles-Louis de Secondat, Baron de Montesquieu. Although he was an innovator of genius and quite probably the creator of modern sociology as well as the great pioneer in its application to political and historical problems, his work is now largely regarded as a mere, if major, document of intellectual history and is seldom consulted for its author's insights into his own society.

Montesquieu's reputation, of course, rests primarily on his intuition that governments derived their form not from logical or moral categories, but rather from general laws in much the same manner as other natural phenomena. He begins, that is, with the law of nature and works down through natural and political to civil law, which he describes as that which regulates the relations among members of the same society in the form of a government. This last, he claims, in his most famous insight, derives its character from that of its population, which in turn is influenced by the climate and other aspects of the environment. According to the particular combination of these factors, government will take one of three principal forms: that of a republic, a monarchy, or a despotism. Thus, instead of deriving his laws from particular situations, he has merely formulated a new set of conventional abstractions, and to illustrate their usefulness, he gathered examples from the ancient world, the Orient, and even the early history of France—but relatively few from his own contemporary Europe. The reasons for this literary discretion are too obvious to require comment, but the results are nonetheless disappointing.

That Montesquieu should have so quickly fallen back into abstractions is not surprising. In addition to writing under the influence of Newton and the law of the spheres, he must also have felt the impact of Grotius and the law of nations. As a professional jurist, well aware of the disorderly confusion of particular laws and constitutions, Montesquieu sought some logical system to organize and explain their bewildering variety. To do this, he established simple, universal categories and then attempted to relate them to the settings in which each appeared.

Before examining this system, which he seems to have drawn more from the air than from his examples, we would do well to remember that the air he breathed was French and to consider his own particular background and experience.

Born to the old, landed nobility of a family that had established its position by devoted service to Henry II of Navarre (grandfather of Henry IV of France), Charles-Louis de Secondat inherited from his father the estate of La Brède, three leagues from Bordeaux, and from his uncle a town house in that city as well as a presidency *à mortier* in its Parlement. Thus, at the same time that he was reared in a tradition of service to the Bourbons, he had roots in the provincial nobility, including a position in its Parlement, and he enjoyed *entrée* to the society of the great port city and membership in its Academy. All of this he left to spend the best part of his adult life in the capital of the realm, as a pampered guest of its salons and a member of its Royal Academy. He must have understood, at least instinctively, all three of the components of the *ancien régime* for which we are searching in his pages: the monarchy and its administrative-military apparatus; the old feudal "residue" that lived on its estates in uneasy truce with the royal bureaucracy; as well as the commercial community of Bordeaux and, through it, much of the Atlantic world. Finally, in Paris he obviously studied, assiduously and at close hand, the administrative center of the monarchical power he so much admired.

Montesquieu's opening distinction among republics, monarchies, and despotisms in the *Esprit des Lois* reveals his principal preoccupation. Republics, he writes, are governments by more than a single ruler. If the rulers are few, it is an aristocracy; if many, a popular democracy. Monarchies are governments by a single ruler, tempered by the restraint of a nobility. Despotisms are the unrestricted rule of one—that is, a monarchy without a nobility. But any government by a single sovereign—whether it consists of one or many—that is unchecked by a second, independent power is, by his definition, a despotism. Therefore, even though he instinctively treats the unlimited authority of a single ruler as despotic authority, he expressly warns against the tyrannical potentialities of popular democracy in Tocquevillian terms.

Each type of government, Montesquieu continues, has its own guiding principle: a republic, virtue; a monarchy, honor; and a despotism, fear. In the case of monarchy, the nobles supply the honor by their desire to serve the king and win his recognition. To be effective, however, a nobility must be independent, which, in practice, means hereditary and privileged. Without such a position to defend, nobles lose their pride and become mere sycophants of a despot. This function of hereditary privilege, moreover, also applies to a republic; without an aristocracy of inherited wealth and position, such a government risks becoming a popular despotism.

All governments, he explains, contain three elements: the legislative, the executive in general, and the executive in particular. About the legislative authority Montesquieu says surprisingly little, except that it makes the laws both temporary and permanent; and without apparent demur, he attributes it to the king in a monarchy or the ruling class in a republic. The second power, the executive that deals with matters that concern the law of nations, consists of the right to make war and peace and otherwise protect the safety of the state. This obviously is to be exercised by the sovereign. It is only the third power, that of judging questions arising from civil law, that Montesquieu hoped to keep separate from monarchical authority and in the hands of an independent nobility.

Although the last of Montesquieu's three powers is usually equated—in English language texts—to the traditional American concept of a separate judiciary, the two are by no means identical. Applied to the *ancien régime*, for example, it would seem to cover much of what, today, would be called local government, as well as the business of the courts; even where it is clearly legal, it is intended to defend liberties at least as much as to render justice. The first two powers, Montesquieu concedes, were exercised by the king and his ministers, not only in France but throughout most of Europe. The third, however, was still jealously guarded by the nobility in France, primarily through the *parlements*, but also by their *de facto* control of local administrative authority even when it was exercised in the name of the king. Montesquieu was aware that the monarchy was eroding this independence, and he indicates that he not only expects the process to continue but that he accepts its ultimate conclusion as a necessary evil. Even so, he warns that, with the judicial power assimilated to the royal government, liberty will be difficult to defend.

The full sense of what Montesquieu means by powers in this doctrine of separation, however, might still be missed by a reader who takes the modern state for granted. In paying tribute to the jurist Gravina for his understanding of the problem, Montesquieu quotes the Italian's revealing phrases: *l'état politique* and *l'état civil*, which he equates with his own executive and judicial powers, respectively. Clearly, he finds nothing amiss in referring to each as an *état*. Moreover, in this context, that slippery word would have to be translated "state." Montesquieu is no apologist for *estates* in either a medieval or sixteenth-century sense. Thus, he not only accepts the idea of two states in a single society, but bases his entire argument on the necessity of such a duality for the preservation of liberty.

In this discussion Montesquieu drops revealing insights about both the character of the nobility and the nature of the monarchy. The king is right, he suggests, to forbid the nobles to involve themselves in commerce, because once they do, they will lose interest in their proper function and become mere businessmen. The *commerçants*, however, who buy titles and become nobles of the robe, adopt the interests of the nobility, which they defend with vigor in their capacity as judges or administrative officials. Not only does this suggest a resolution for a recent academic debate about the nature of the nobility; but it also indicates that Montesquieu saw both these social categories as living and developing organisms within the body politic. This impression is further reinforced by his insistence on the hereditary character of noble privilege and his implied defense of Boulainvilliers' argument buttressed by his dictum that neither the ancient world nor the Orient ever produced a true nobility.

Continuing his consideration of commerce, he states that in a monarchy it will be largely confined to luxuries—apparently for the gratification of the court—and he argues against its extension to more mundane products. The cultivation of grain for local consumption, he maintains, is far more appropriate to a monarchy than, for example, the raising of wool for sale, because it will support more people. Clearly, he is here describing the subsistence agriculture that formed the basis of the monarchy in eighteenth-century France; and, at least by implication, he seems to be formulating a similar correlation between commerce and republics. Curiously, however, in reviewing the nature and role of commerce, he says almost as little about England as he does about France in his discussion of subsistence agriculture. Instead, he draws his examples from the ancient world, the Mediterranean, and particularly the Low Countries.

Montesquieu finds his models of republican government primarily in cities—although the Swiss present an anomalous exception—and the cities he describes are generally commercial. If Rome was a major exception, it at least had the excellent sense to favor, and ultimately profit from, the commerce of others. He also notes the tendency of cities to form leagues, and he discusses some of the problems of federative government. The possibility of nonterritorial, nonadministrative society does not seem to have occurred to him; but the manner in which he organizes and presents his material strongly suggests that he sensed much the same distinction between commercial and agricultural social systems that has been developed in the preceding chapters of this essay. With our contemporary vocabulary at his disposal, he might well have discussed "societies" and their characteristic forms of "government."

Montesquieu's famous misunderstanding of the English constitution was if no less serious at least quite different than it is usually represented. He obviously had grasped the nature of the different institutions that composed the English government, but misjudged their interrelations because he assumed they were independent. He seems to have missed the degree to which the executive (administrative) authority of the king depended on the power of the purse wielded by the Commons and the extent to which the judicial prerogative of the courts was subject to control by the Lords. In practice, the principal separation that existed within the English government seems to have been between functions; and power would appear to have rested ultimately in Parliament. In spite of the royal title of its executive officer, England was, as befitted a commercial community, a republic rather than a monarchy in the continental sense.

On the other hand, Montesquieu's most critical failure was in his treatment of the legislative power. By assigning it to the king in a monarchy, he misread the situation in France. As the events that precipitated the Revolution would later demonstrate, and as Montesquieu should have known from his experience in the *parlement*, the liberties of the nobles depended quite as much on their ability to resist the legislative as the executive authority. The monarchy was essentially administrative and, under normal circumstances, had little need for legislation, which may have diverted attention from the fact that it lacked any real capacity to impose new laws. Montesquieu did seem to recognize, however, that the legislative function was especially important in resolving the affairs of commercial societies. He comments with warm approval, for example, on the flexibility displayed by the English government in setting tariff levels, but he does not quite recognize the integral relations developed among the commercial societies of the Atlantic littoral in the eighteenth century.

Montesquieu's analysis was more remarkable for its intuitive insights than for its inaccuracies, particularly in the light of the almost total lack of comprehension of English society demonstrated by so many of the *philosophes*. Perhaps his initiation into the Atlantic society, in Bordeaux, gave him some instinctive understanding of the English; but, for the most part, he—like so many enlightened continentals, from Voltaire on—regarded them as almost as exotic as the semi-mythical Persians or Chinese: appropriate subjects for cautionary tales.

Given the facts of geographical proximity, facility of travel, and essentially common history, at least from the eleventh through the fifteenth centuries, this sense of difference is astonishing. Even more surprising, however, is the lack of comment on, let alone the effort to explain, this remarkable phenomenon. Today it is taken for granted that the intellectual and cultural styles of England and Europe are separated by an unbridgeable Channel. How or why this came about no one seems to ask, but it can be established without much difficulty that this separation occurred precisely in the seventeenth and eighteenth centuries. Is it possible that this transformation was in some sense a consequence of the emergence of a new and discrete social structure, based on the equally new commercial economy of the Atlantic cities?

Another way to look at the problem would be through English eyes. Did the English themselves recognize their divergence from the society and culture of the Continent? Certainly they had ample opportunity to get to know it with their endless traveling, whether in the grand tours of the rich or the wanderings of skilled craftsmen. One thing that became increasingly obvious to inhabitants of both countries, during the course of the eighteenth century, was the growing disproportion of wealth in England's favor. Not only did English commerce vastly exceed that of France, but so did English industry and even English agriculture. Although the real reasons for these striking and mounting discrepancies were by no means fully understood, attempts at explanation were offered, and of these the most important was Adam Smith's *Wealth of Nations*.

Written to argue that wealth was created by the circulation of goods, not by the protection of markets for the purpose of accumulating money, as the mercantilists maintained, this text also provided an idealized description of the operation of the commercial economy of the Atlantic. Smith does not labor the role of water transport, because he assumes its availability; but he may not have been fully aware of the degree to which the Continent lacked a system of natural canals such as that provided by English rivers. Not merely did England's insular position force her to conduct all foreign commerce overseas, but her deep-sided rivers brought half her territory within practical reach of navigable water. Given the nature of the society in which he lived, and about which he was writing, Smith's strictures on mercantilism are both perceptive and well founded. Applied to the subsistence agriculture of rural France, however, their relevance or applicability is less clear, raising the question of whether the great ministers and intendants of the French crown were as completely misguided in their mercantilist policies as has generally been assumed. Although the need for capital was urgent, the economic base of the monarchy was not ocean commerce but continental agriculture. Possibly the French king could have made more money by moving to Bordeaux and staking his future on its fortunes in Atlantic commerce, but that was simply not his business. Of his twenty-five million subjects, at least twenty million were peasants; another half million, more or less, were country nobles, and of the urban dwellers, at least half inhabited inland market towns and provincial capitals. Virtually all of these diverse groups lived in and by the military-administrative-agricultural system that comprised the monarchy. Even if the nobles maintained an anachronistic independence of the royal fisc, they were inextricably tied to the land, and many served in the army. If anything, they were even more remote from the new ocean community than the rest of the population.

A striking illustration of the difference between these systems, as well as the difficulty of translating the experience of one to the practice of the other, is provided by the theories and activities of the Physiocrats. This remarkable group, comprising the most important French economists of the *ancien régime,* was led by François Quesnay. Once established at Versailles, as the personal physician of the royal favorite, Madame de Pompadour, that unusual physician turned his restless and incisive mind to the distempers of the realm, which he saw as economic. Not only did he direct the work of his disciples, but he corresponded widely with other economists, including Adam Smith, who was sufficiently attracted by Quesnay and his theories to visit him in France.

It requires no detailed analysis of Physiocratic doctrine to say that it derived largely from two sources. The first was Quesnay's clear understanding that the French economy was based on agriculture, essentially the production of wheat, and the second was Adam Smith's theory of commerce. Putting the two together, Quesnay and his followers launched a powerful campaign to free grain of all traditional trade restrictions and local tariffs. Once liberated, they argued, production and sales would increase, adding not only to the well-being of the people, but to the wealth of the state as well. This program was eventually implemented by Turgot, with results that were not only immediate and unexpected, but almost as disastrous for France as they were for the great intendant himself. Grain prices soared, scarcities and panics ensued, and only the swift restoration of the old controls saved the country from a major crisis.

In spite of wide and continuing interest in Quesnay's theoretical work, the reason for the failure of his program has not been entirely resolved. One obvious explanation, however, seems to be that he attempted to apply theories and techniques developed within the oceanic community to French agricultural society. Removing the restrictions from the grain trade, it turned out, did not increase its circulation, at least not in any normal commercial manner, because of the cost and difficulty of transport. There was therefore no possibility of creating the vast new inland market that Quesnay had predicted. Instead of increasing production, the reform provoked panic buying, which drove prices up and induced a dangerous if artificial shortage. Obviously the old market controls and internal tariff regulations had served some other purpose than that of merely collecting revenues for the crown.

Many of these restrictions could, in fact, be traced to the fourteenth century, when a series of disastrous famines drove local communities to prohibit outside sale of their own inadequate grain supplies. In any situation of widespread starvation, the price of food loses all relation to intrinsic costs of production or transportation. Advanced societies have now learned that salvation in such circumstances as, for example, a state of war or siege depends on rigorous control of price and distribution; and it was to these devices that the desperate victims of the universal crop failures of the fourteenth century had resorted. Apparently unaware of the origin of the restrictions he attacked, Quesnay obviously understood neither their purpose nor their implications. No shrewd observer of the eighteenth century could have missed the fact that starvation was still endemic, and Quesnay less than most; but he seems to have attributed the chronic shortage of grain to the existing taxes and restrictions on its circulation. That is why he expected the removal of the latter to correct the former and thus, by a single stroke, to increase both the country's food supply and its general prosperity.

In eighteenth-century Europe, grain was in chronic short supply; the growing towns and cities placed a steadily increasing pressure on available sources of food. The commercial cities, of course, fed themselves by importing grain from coastal, or riverside, plantations such as those in East Prussia, while cities of the hinterland fostered local plantation farming, thus vastly increasing the value of adjacent land. Important as this internal urban market was, however, it significantly did not transform the bulk of inland agriculture into a commercial venture. The large majority of the population still lived essentially by subsistence farming; and because grain could not be moved economically and efficiently over land, there was little incentive in most areas to increase production. That Quesnay's efforts to free this nonexistent trade backfired in so spectacular a manner seems to have been due, at least in part, to the constantly recurring local crop failures that maintained a panic market for grain. Since these shortages occurred irregularly and unforeseeably, they did not create a constant, predictable demand in any given area. When supply failed, those with money were ready to pay the normally prohibitive costs of transport as well as premium prices. This grim fact of life in eighteenth-century France introduced an irrational factor into the country's economy that Quesnay failed to take into account in his insightful but highly abstract analysis.

To have solved the food problem or to have made Quesnay's program work, far more than the abolition of taxes and trade restrictions would have been required. Much of the old traditional subsistence farming would have had to be replaced by commercial plantations, which in turn would have involved two revolutionary steps, both quite beyond the imagination and resources of the time. First, a cheap, efficient internal transport system would have had to be devised. Probably this would have meant an extended system of canals, which, in a country as large and varied as France, was a staggering concept. Even if some important efforts were made to develop inland water transport, often with considerable success; nothing on a scale adequate to revolutionize the country's agriculture was ever considered, let alone undertaken. Second, the transformation of the subsistence economy into a system of plantations would have involved the transfer of a significant segment of the rural population to towns or cities. The whole point of commercial farming is to produce a far larger surplus with a much smaller work force than would be normal in a subsistence situation. In the second half of the twentieth century, the modernization and rationalization of French agriculture has meant the drastic reduction of the country's farm labor force. In the eighteenth century, such a transformation was, if not quite unthinkable, certainly considered undesirable, as the famous literature of the "populationists" attests. The Physiocrats, therefore, in spite of their surprising grasp of the principles of a commercial economy, had not fully taken the measure of the difficulties the implementation of either inland transportation or population relocation would involve in France. Moreover, their conviction that agriculture was the only true source of economic value suggests they did not fully grasp the implications of large-scale commerce for either methods of production or patterns of social organization. What they did appreciate was the role of subsistence farming in France.

In his greatly admired economic model, "Le Tableau économique," Quesnay himself appears to be demonstrating that only money circulated; but whether he understood that the monarchy, not commerce, was the mechanism by which this worked in his own society is not clear. In any case, the Physiocratic experiment serves once again to illustrate, and in a dramatic fashion, the difficulty that members of one society had in understanding the nature, or even the existence, of the other. Quesnay had a remarkable insight into the nature of the monarchy as a fiscal institution; but if he also sensed the logical superiority of Adam Smith's theory of commerce, he seems not to have fully grasped the unbridgeable differences between the oceanic and continental economies.

Reactions, whether in public criticism or official reports, to the fiscal crisis that increasingly threatened the monarchy in the last quarter of the eighteenth century almost all assumed a realistic view of the social structure of France. Tax reform was recognized to be the only means of raising the royal revenue sufficiently to service the existing debt and to reverse the disastrous course of deficit financing by ever-increasing loans. The bureaucratic machinery, an antiquated product of continued improvisation, was patently unequal to its task; but so was the tax structure. Not only were the kingdom's largest landowners exempt from the basic tax on land, but the rest of the population were assessed unequally and, even worse, the exactions served as a retributive penalty of visible progress or prosperity. In different ways and to different degrees, most of the great officers of the crown recognized that the salvation of the monarchy depended on a thorough reform of this antiquated, inadequate, and pernicious system. The obvious measures to be taken were to remove collection from the private hands of the Farmers General and transfer it to the officers of the state, reduce or eliminate the fiscal exemptions of the privileged orders, and standardize rates and procedures of collection. If some critics stressed one or another of these three, the best informed agreed that all were necessary and, ultimately, inevitable.

Even though the nature and solution of the problem were well understood, the practical difficulties in the way of effective reform were great. First, to extricate the monarchy from the toils of the Farmers General would require a massive transfusion of capital that, under existing conditions, could come only from that same banking fraternity. In other words, refunding the royal debt without reforming the fisc would be a meaningless exercise. Furthermore, the bankers themselves were under mounting and contradictory pressures to increase as well as defend their investment in the crown. In the eighteenth century, commercial profits had burgeoned far beyond existing possibilities of private reinvestment. In this situation, the royal debt was a unique institution, the only one to which the bankers could turn to unload their rapidly accumulating capital. They were thus driven to make ever larger loans to the monarchy, while the increasing insecurity of royal credit drove them to greater and greater concern over the inadequacies of the fiscal administration. If they were under all but irresistible pressure to go on lending to the bankrupt king, far beyond the level that his revenues could service or justify, the increasing vulnerability of their investment made them correspondingly aware of the importance of maintaining their control of the Tax Farms. For the royal administrators to move against these outmoded institutions, therefore, was to risk cutting their line of credit, and this the monarchy could not afford, even for a brief interval.

To proceed by the abolition of tax privileges, as some of the great royal officials recommended, would hardly have been more feasible. Any such measure would have dealt the country nobility a mortal blow; and however irrational and anachronistic their position was, the nobles were too strongly entrenched to be liquidated by mere administrative action, as one minister after another learned. For one thing, the nobility provided the entire officer corps for the army, and even though a substantial number of the lesser nobles had undoubtedly shifted their allegiance to the monarchy, the king would have had to think very carefully before trying to move against aristocratic privileges by military force. Moreover, the more affluent nobles of the robe who dominated the *parlements,* and through them the judicial system, used this position to defend the integral privileges of their caste. Finally, the upper clergy was composed entirely of nobles; and even if the church was theoretically subject to the crown in France, the king could hardly have ignored the threat of massive clerical opposition.

Given the strength of the nobles' position, it is perhaps surprising to find them, or at least their privileges, under such vigorous and coherent attack as the regime drifted toward its debacle. Leadership in this campaign was provided by the great administrators of the crown, but able and well trained as they were, they lacked any independent political base of their own. Increasingly, they were supported by a host of lesser apologists who had begun to appear throughout the country. In the market towns and small administrative centers a new class of bourgeois (that is, non-noble) lawyers had grown up to defend the interests of the provincial members of the monarchical society. It was they who seem to have suffered most, or at least most consciously, from the delaying and obfuscating tactics of the aristocratic courts and therefore best understood the pall that privilege cast over all administrative efforts at reform. Through the famous corresponding societies, these provincial critics exchanged ideas and laid the intellectual foundation for much that happened in 1789 and after.

Although in quite a different way, the intellectuals of the court and capital, including many of the ministers, also tended to take the side of monarchical reform against established practice. Granting the utter incongruity of the nobles' position, it is not surprising that it should have become the favorite target of social critics and reformers, any more than it is strange that the most enlightened public servants should have attempted to deal with the problem by administrative (that is, authoritarian) action. The very rationality of these reactions, however, has tended to divert attention from the fact that right in the middle of what has been described as the "democratic revolution," an entire generation of gifted social critics and publicists should all but unanimously demand the royal imposition of their various programs of reform. In the theoretical and polemical literature of the time, the "absolute" monarchy was criticized for its failure to exercise arbitrary power. To Frenchmen of the *ancien régime*, it was the monarchy that represented what was modern and progressive; and political "liberties" that appeared anachronistic.

While it might be possible to attribute part of this reaction to personal ambition in a situation in which the monarchy was virtually the only ladder to fame and fortune, it must also have been due to an understanding of the social-economic structure of the country. For virtually all the inhabitants of continental France, fiscal and judicial reforms were far more urgent issues than the development of political liberty; and the monarchy was the obvious agency for their implementation. Only the king's failure to live up to their expectations drove his subjects to intervene. Because their action emanated from the nation and was aimed at the welfare of the common citizen, it was considered democratic; but it neither depended on nor developed those representative or legislative institutions of government that are now traditionally associated with that word in the English-speaking world. In eighteenth-century Europe, however, there was more concern for equal-handed and efficient administration than popular participation in government. The royal administrators fully understood that the prosperity of the kingdom depended on the well-being of the peasants; and it was on this basic concept that Napoleon was to build his Empire. There is little evidence to suggest that the Whig lords of England—in spite of their liberal political ideas—felt the need to concern themselves with the fate of the urban proletariat of their port cities. If population pressure continued to provide an adequate supply of labor, they would be able to prosper without considering the plight of their victims. And their successors, the industrial entrepreneurs of the next century, would find themselves in the same "fortunate" position.

That this generally coherent view of French problems, and the manner in which they might be solved, was widely held in France on the eve of the Revolution is amply attested to, not merely by the pamphlet and other critical literature of the pre-Revolutionary period, but also by the *cahiers,* or lists of grievances drawn up by each electoral circumscription at the same time it chose its deputy to the Estates General in 1789. As is well known, virtually no direct attacks on the institution of the monarchy were to be found in that vast accumulation of documentary evidence. This discordant note of constitutional, legislative, and representative government was introduced early in the deliberations of the Estates by spokesmen for the bankers and merchants of the commercial ports, who would rapidly acquire the fitting name of "Girondins." Clearly they understood the nature of English (Atlantic) legislative government and believed they required something of the sort to enable them not merely to resolve the fiscal crisis, but also to provide a continuing supervisory control of royal finance. What never occurred to them, until too late, was that it was not their revolution. Their assumption that the demonstrated inadequacy of the administrative monarchy gave them the right to dismantle and replace it by a simple "constitutional" model was based in a fundamental ignorance of the true nature of the realm.

The first and decisive problem the Girondins encountered was that the bulk of the country's revolutionaries did not understand either their language or objectives. The provincial radicals sensed that the constitutional monarchy would result in a reinforcement of the country aristocracy because of Mirabeau's insistence on a royal veto and a second legislative house. With Montesquieu, Mirabeau believed that the English government was spared the threat of despotism by the distribution of its power among three independent institutions, any one of which could be checked by the other two. In this context both saw a "House of Peers" as a necessary curb on either royal or popular authority, without sensing in the slightest what it would mean to rural France. But too many woes of the countryside had derived from the supposedly "second estate" of the nobility, which can now be seen as a separate, hostile, and anachronistic social residue. Thus for the majority of the members of the National Assembly, the reconstitution of an upper house did not guarantee political freedom from monarchical despotism, but the reimposition of illogical and pernicious privilege. Those who understood the English government hoped to use it as a model for a new governing body to provide the administrative monarchy with competent and responsible fiscal supervision. But in projecting a French "House of Lords," they were thinking of Whig (that is, financial or commercial) oligarchs, not of reactionary feudal landlords. Unable to grasp this distinction, the rural reformers took it for granted that any such institution in France in 1790 would be, not a curb on despotic authority, but an instrument of feudal reaction.

As any student of the period knows, the revolutionary agenda of the *cahiers* found its full expression in the Napoleonic Empire. Virtually every public institution in France was reformed and rationalized between 1789 and 1806, and much of the new administrative apparatus was extended to the conquered territories. Particularly striking was the effort to integrate the economy of Europe in the Continental System, which, for all its provisions for trade, was still based primarily on subsistence agriculture. In effecting the reforms outlined in the *cahiers* and initiated by the Directory, Napoleon came close to fulfilling the eighteenth-century ideal of an enlightened despot. Even his military activity was only an exaggerated version of one of the necessary attributes of the traditional philosopher-king. The monarchy was a military organization, and the army an essential part of the economy. It is no accident that Napoleon's wars finally opened careers to talent on a large enough scale to meet what had perhaps been the most explosive demand of the entire revolutionary program. No existing institution was capable of providing an adequate outlet for the pent-up energies of the population, as Stendhal was to testify with such eloquence in the opening pages of *The Red and the Black*. The Empire, in short, was the apogee of the agricultural monarchy and the end product of a revolution intended to perfect, not subvert, that institution.

That Napoleon had at least an innate understanding of his relation to the monarchy as well as to the Revolution is suggested by his search, launched in 1804, for a historian to trace the developments, from the *ancien régime* through the Revolution, that culminated in the new hereditary monarchy or empire he was constructing. The theme was to be the unity of the national history, and the purpose to unite rival factions around the new government. Although Napoleon did not find it easy to identify a qualified scholar who shared his vision, he did eventually find one willing to accept the assignment. Improbably, his candidate came from the ranks of the ex-*émigrés*, and perhaps predictably, the work he finally produced failed to meet the Emperor's specifications. The author, the Comte de Montlosier, had taken a long view of his subject and had treated it as the story of the struggle between two rival segments of the French people.

Although Montlosier's treatment unmistakably evoked the Boulainvilliers thesis, it was translated into more sophisticated terms. In place of a simple concept of race, he conjured up what amounts to a theory of class. The original Franks are reinforced by enfranchised individuals selected from among the subject Gallo-Roman masses. Recruited on a sort of merit system, these new "Franks" prevented the nobility from hardening into a closed hereditary caste and preserved its character of an open elite. Under the extreme social and financial pressure generated by the Crusades, however, the system broke down, and large numbers of the subject population were enfranchised with little or no preparation. As a result, the new, expanded "establishment" of the monarchy itself was now divided between the true elite and the *nouveaux arrivés* still clinging to their old servile professions and prejudices.

Because the nobles had needed money, a commodity they normally could live without, for the Crusades, they had had to turn to the townsmen for assistance. This put the latter in a position to buy their freedom from feudal obligations, which they did too rapidly and on too large a scale to be assimilated into the aristocracy. Instead, they became an anti-aristocracy, vying with the nobles for power, attacking their standards as well as their position and, in general, subverting the moral and social order of the country. The climax of this struggle was the Revolution, in which the "new people" seized all the power, and while blaming the nobles for all the ills and injustices of the past, reshaped France in their own image. But even if they had succeeded in sweeping away the monarchy, in their triumph, it seemed to Montlosier that they had received a setback with the emergence of the Empire and the restoration of titles which offered the old nobles an opportunity to open an offensive.

When Napoleon finally saw the manuscript in 1807, he was understandably disappointed and prevented its publication. As soon as it appeared in 1814, however, it at once became the bible of the Ultras, the prime target of the Liberals, and the effective source of the persistent myth of a France divided against itself by the Revolution. Moreover, because its author was not exactly clear about the nature of his elite—whether it was essentially a caste or a class—his theory was to survive the social and economic changes of the nineteenth century, to reappear in the twentieth in the guise of Beau de Loménie's Marxist monarchism that combined both definitions.

The life-and-death struggle around which Montlosier developed his account was unmistakably—in the terms already defined in the preceding chapters—between the emerging administrative monarchy and the surviving feudal nobles. Montlosier's charge of treason against the King has a quaint, nostalgic ring, but his characterization of the towns and their citizens is excellent. What he misses, however, is any clear sense of the existence, let alone implications, of the commercial community of the great peripheral cities. His goal, in fact, was not essentially different from that of Napoleon in that he wished to reunite and reorganize agricultural France. Montlosier even conceded the necessity of a strong king to achieve this end; but the ultimate objective was the restoration of the "old" nobles to a position of power and prestige. Napoleon, of course, understood better than anyone that the unity of the inner country depended on the monarchy (or emperor) and that the nobles had ceased to exist as an independent force. He had offered them all he could: the fictitious role of ornamenting his court.

Alexis de Tocqueville's famous strictures against the old monarchy in his *Ancien régime* merely follow out this lead. His overriding concern was the continuing institutional threat it posed to the traditional liberties of the realm, as he termed the anachronistic privileges of his aristocratic predecessors. Furthermore, in his famous visit to and study of America, he foresaw the implications of truly democratic participation in an administrative state. Whether he was correct in assuming that the United States would inevitably develop such a central administration is at least open to discussion, but that he accurately measured the implications of full democracy within the monarchical structure of France is clear.

Since there is no evidence, however, that he appreciated the significance of the impending industrial revolution or even really understood the existing commercial-capitalist system, his prophetic concern for the future retains a pastoral, archaic tone. During the wartime isolation of the Continent, England's commercial economy was escalated to a new industrial level, correspondingly increasing all the differences and difficulties that had always existed between the two societies. The French ports became mere hangers-on in the Atlantic commerce; and until inland transportation itself was industrialized, there was no possibility of effecting a true industrial revolution in France. Even with the gradual industrialization of the Continent by the introduction of the railroad in the mid-nineteenth century, the old agricultural society continued to coexist with the new. In the case of France, the story of the relations between the two is the key to the country's political history since the close of the Revolution.

It would appear, from this canvass, that at least some of the ablest political critics or practitioners of the eighteenth and early nineteenth centuries understood the socio-economic structure of the agricultural monarchy in France. A few also recognized, from personal experience, the continual persistence of a residual feudal society in the country nobles and their characteristic institution, the *parlements*. Hardly any, however, really understood the Atlantic community. Montesquieu seems to have had some apprehension of its existence, but he certainly did not produce a clear description of its organization. Adam Smith, who formulated the classic analysis of its economic operation, did not treat it as a discrete social system; and the Physiocrats, who obviously wanted to apply his doctrine to the French economy, failed to grasp the significance of the oceanic base of commerce. Instead, they revealed some remarkable insights into the nature of the monarchical economy of France itself.

Altogether, it would seem reasonable to conclude that the social structure of agricultural France was well enough understood, but that the less tangible Atlantic community was difficult for minds, accustomed to the territorial state, to grasp. It did not occur to members of the commercial society to propose their social-economic system as a concrete alternative to the state, because they knew they neither possessed nor wanted a total administrative government on the continental model. What they enjoyed, they had no need to describe; and their alien critics had no eyes to see—let alone understand. It was this failure of comprehension that has made the politics and history of France in the seventeenth and eighteenth centuries so misleading, and in the nineteenth and twentieth so puzzling.

CHAPTER FIVE

The Other France

———————•———————

THE THREE discrete societies proposed and described in the preceding chapters as the component elements of pre-Revolutionary France do not explain the social and political cleavages that plagued the country in the nineteenth and twentieth centuries. Not only was the Revolution produced by the conflict of interests and an imbalance of forces among these coeval and contending structures, but it resulted, directly or indirectly, in their elimination or transformation. Within a few months of the meeting of the Estates General, the old feudal society was dissolved; and in the ensuing wars with England, the port cities were largely cut off from the Atlantic community and its commerce. Because of this, the merchant bankers were unable to maintain their independent existence, but they did manage to save some of their capital by investing it in church lands or army contracts. With both the feudal and commercial societies apparently destroyed and their members in exile or in hiding, the land seemed cleared of obstacles to the formation of a single coherent nation-state. Indeed, Napoleon believed, or at least hoped, that he had already accomplished this goal in the first decade of the century. His claim, however, was not only challenged by Montlosier and a large majority of the post-Revolutionary critics, but increasingly belied by the subsequent history of the century.

It was Napoleon's revival of titles and the gradual return of the *émigrés* that caught the public's attention; but it was the re-emergence of the bankers, beginning in the Directorate, that was to lead to the formation of a new rival society. As *notables* of the Empire, they moved—after Napoleon's abdication—into positions that allowed them to arrange the Restoration with astonishing ease. At this stage they probably constituted little more than a powerful clique, concerned for their investment in the state; but with the return of peace they began to find other ways to place their funds. If they never recovered their previous position in the Atlantic community, they did return to commerce, but in a new role, as the importers of England's industrial revolution. Before the middle of the century, inland transport in the form of railroads had become a more important investment than ocean commerce; and even before that, significant amounts of capital were being placed in factory installations throughout the hinterland. These were normally located in provincial cities, transforming some of the old crafts into new industries and thereby creating a new capitalist urban society that had surprisingly little contact with the surrounding communities that still lived by subsistence agriculture. Even after the railroads were built, the two continued to coexist and maintain their separate identities well into the twentieth century.

As a result, within eighty odd years after the Revolution, a completely new economic community emerged; but it did so within the old, though reconstituted, agricultural society. These two structures that have controlled life in France since the Revolution thus took shape well before the onset of either the transportation or industrial revolutions; and when these finally occurred, they developed within, and largely conformed to, established social patterns. Industrialization, that is, did not modernize France to the degree it did Germany or the United States in the second half of the century, precisely because it failed to break out of, let alone transform, the existing social structures. Instead, it gradually developed new, self-contained capitalist communities in the urban interstices of the old agricultural society, which, in spite of the sweeping reforms of the Revolution, still maintained an administrative state on the subsistence base.

To trace the development of this new society, it is necessary to return to the deepening fiscal crisis of the 1780's. On the surface, this was a confused struggle between the great nobles and great bankers as to who should pay for the impending royal bankruptcy. For some time, ministers and intendants had been advocating a total revision of the country's fiscal system that would equalize the assessment and rationalize the collection of taxes. Nothing less drastic than the elimination of noble exemptions would increase revenues sufficiently to bring the royal debt back into manageable proportion. But this immediate problem was only a surface manifestation of a continuing struggle between the monarchy and nobility for the right to exploit the peasantry, which was currently being crushed by the combination of royal taxes and feudal dues. The gravity of the situation had come to obsess the country's intellectuals, from the *philosophes* to the members of small-town corresponding societies. Reform and even revolution, thanks to the popular American model, were the subjects of the day.

The King proved incapable of the resolution necessary to master the situation. Characteristically he would appoint a reformer like Calonne but not support his program against the vociferous opposition of the nobles. Sensing Louis' weakness, these latter attempted to reinforce their position *vis-à-vis* the crown, without considering the impact of their action on the public at large. When the King summoned an Assembly of Notables in 1787, the representatives of the nobility refused to ratify any concessions and demanded the convocation of a full Estates General. Their strategy was obvious. When that moribund institution had last met with any regularity in the sixteenth century, it had sat and voted in three separate orders, the First, or Clergy; the Second, or Nobility; and the Third, essentially the bourgeoisie. Because the upper clergy were all nobles, they followed the lead of the Second, and together they regularly outvoted the Third. In practice this meant that commoners who needed the King to impose some order on the nobility were forced to support him with their own funds.

Clearly, the nobles intended to replay this old script in 1789. They assumed the Estates would be elected and organized according to the ancient usage, giving them an effective veto of dangerous reforms and leaving the bankers to cope with the problem of the debt with their fellow members of the Third. What did not occur to them was that once the Estates had been assembled, they would no longer be sparring with vulnerable bankers but confronting an aroused nation. Since the deputies to the Third were to be elected by what amounted to universal manhood suffrage, they would draw their mandate overwhelmingly from the hinterland. Even though the peasants probably took little part in drafting their parish *cahiers* and sent no direct representatives to Versailles, the small-town lawyers who dominated the Third came largely from the agricultural community. Few businessmen were elected, even in the port-city delegations, and such champions of the great financial interests as appeared hardly constituted a major group. The overwhelming majority of the deputies of the Third came from rural France and were preoccupied with the rationalization of the monarchy.

From the first mention of an Estates General, spokesmen for the Third demanded twice as many deputies as either the First or Second. Patently there was no sense in such a provision, unless the Estates were to vote by head, as was done in some provincial assemblies, rather than by order, as the nobles intended they should. The King temporized, giving the Third its six hundred deputies and then accepting the nobles' demand that the orders be maintained; but the Third, fully aware of the decisive implications of this ruling, refused to meet alone. After a brief stalemate, they were joined by the lower clergy, who, because they came from and lived among the peasants, shared many of the aims of the commoners. Confronted with a *fait accompli,* the King countered with the futile gesture of closing the meeting hall "for repairs," and provoked the determined reformers to the revolutionary defiance of the Tennis Court Oath. With this dramatic gesture they assumed not only the necessary authority to implement their program, but the responsibility for regularizing the exercise of the nation's sovereign rights in a constitution.

The significance of their step is easy to overlook. By now, it is taken more or less for granted that the purpose of revolutions is to replace old constitutions with new, but constitutional reform did not figure significantly in the original revolutionary agenda of 1789. In spite of the fact that the concept of constitution was widely familiar, thanks to the much discussed and admired American model as well as the political literature of the

Continent, it had been invoked in the pre-Revolutionary debate chiefly by the nobles, who had based their defense on the traditional or unwritten constitution of which they claimed to be custodians. The *cahiers,* however, reveal far more concern with the rationalization of the administrative regime than the reform of the political structure. The reformers, that is, were much more concerned about the quality than the character of government. They were more interested in being governed well than in governing themselves. There was little serious disagreement or debate about what was needed to set the kingdom right, and a series of royal ministers had decreed the desired reforms. It was the King's failure to override the resistance that had necessitated the calling of the Estates and then his desultory and halfhearted campaign of obstruction that provoked this crisis and forced the reformers to assert their supremacy over the crown.

With its assumption of sovereignty, the National Assembly accepted three simultaneous obligations: first, to conduct the day-to-day affairs of the realm; second, to implement reform; and finally, to draft a new constitution. From the outset their deliberations were not merely accompanied but influenced by momentous events. The seizure and destruction of the Bastille by the Paris mob was a warning to King and nobles not to try to use the army. The concurrent and continuing rural uprisings, known as the Great Fear, demonstrated to a horrified nobility that reform could no longer be forestalled by mere inaction. In a famous night session of the Assembly, the nobles responded to this crisis by renouncing one after another of their hereditary privileges; and although much has been made of their subsequent effort to recover some of the concessions, the trend they set proved irreversible, leading ultimately to the complete dissolution of their order.

Other measures, such as the dismantling of the provinces, together with their administrative and judicial apparatus, as well as the confiscation of the church lands and the establishment of a civil constitution for the clergy, speeded the process of dissolving aristocratic prerogatives toward its inevitable conclusion. With the provincial institutions went the nobles' principal bastions of defense; and with the church lands, they lost an important source of sinecures and influence. When the Republic administered the *coup de grâce* by outlawing their titles and confiscating their estates, the nobles had already been reduced to the legal status of ordinary, if more or less affluent, citizens. And although a surprising number were able to retain or re-acquire significant portions of their land, they had clearly lost that independent character, based in hereditary privilege, which Montesquieu had insisted was essential to their corporate existence.

Ironically, these measures may actually have benefited the miserable *hobereaux* who constituted the large majority of the order. Condemned by the taboos of their caste to eschew gainful employment, and by the exigency of their poverty to serve as ill-paid junior officers in the army of their King, derogation for them must have been a liberation. Napoleon himself came from this group and without the Revolution could never have risen above the rank of major. But whether individual nobles viewed the abolition of their special status as loss or gain, there would appear to be no room for doubt that it had been abolished once and for all. The restoration of privilege in any legal or fiscal sense was never seriously contemplated, even by the majority of the surviving nobles, who realized the outburst such a suggestion would have provoked.

While, as events revealed, the liquidation of the nobility had been the first and most urgent item of the revolutionary agenda, the reconstitution of royal authority had not figured in it at all. None of the deputies to the Third Estate had arrived at Versailles with ill-will toward their King, and most probably asked nothing better than that he lead them in their task of remaking France. Quite possibly a brighter, more purposeful monarch might have accepted the crisis as an opportunity not only to implement long-overdue reforms, but also to strengthen his own position at the expense of the first two estates. Had not the monarchy been built by just such cooperation between king and commoners in the past? Louis' ambivalence and indecision, however, dissipated this possibility and forced the Assembly not merely to assume but to define his unfulfilled responsibilities. As a result, during the same period that the nobility was being extirpated from the social and political fabric of the realm, the deputies set about constructing a new constitution for the nation. It was this exercise that produced the decisive confrontation between the two remaining societies: the administrative and the commercial.

Because the constitutional monarchy could not be made to work and ended in disaster, it has become traditional to charge its authors and supporters with political inexperience. Professor Robert K. Gooch has argued, however, that the deputies who seized the initiative in this area demonstrated a surprisingly keen understanding of the nature and problems of constitutional monarchy, as it was then practiced in its classic form in England. What they did not understand was the revolution that was taking place in France. Following their notorious but gifted leader, Honoré Gabriel Mirabeau, they tried to establish the essential institutions for a parliamentary government. To defend the principle of an independent executive they advocated a royal veto; and to balance the unlimited authority of a single assembly they proposed a second chamber. But the majority of the deputies, being much less sensitive to constitutional refinements than social and administrative reforms, saw the veto as an attempt to reinforce the position of a proved opponent of their revolutionary gains and a House of Peers as a mere trick to revive the hated nobles. Not until the entire revolutionary agenda was finally implemented by Napoleon, was France ready to accept the kind of constitutional monarchy that Mirabeau and his followers in the National Assembly had attempted to create.

Initially, no one in the National Assembly opposed a monarchy; and all agreed on the necessity of a constitution. Only a minority, however, really understood or wanted a constitutional monarchy; and when the nature and implications of that institution finally permeated the consciousness of the others, it became the major issue that polarized the two remaining political forces in France under the now classic names of Girondins and Jacobins. In recent years it has been fashionable to make light of the connections between the first of these famous parties and the region of the Bordelais, but that their contemporaries thought of them in these terms should not be too quickly dismissed. Further, the unswerving devotion of the Girondins to the concept of limited authority, in the teeth of mounting difficulties and resistance, seems to separate them in a fundamental fashion from their Jacobin opponents. In fact, it was to provide the Jacobins with the excuse to force the Girondins from power. Having blundered into war under the illusion that either victory or defeat would diffuse the Revolution, the Girondin ministry suffered reverse after reverse, inevitably providing the Jacobins with ammunition to attack not only their revolutionary will, but more importantly their political and military capacity as well.

The final crisis was provoked by the discovery of the King's treasonable correspondence with the enemy. At his trial, not even the Girondins tried to save him from conviction; but while voting for his condemnation, however, they opposed his execution, not so much to spare Louis as to salvage the principle of constitutional monarchy. For the Jacobins, however, his treason to the Revolution convinced them they could never entrust the monarchy to another king and drove them to destroy the royal office, together with its hapless incumbent, and to declare the Republic.

Besides setting the course of the Revolution, this confrontation also served to confuse all subsequent political terminology in France by establishing the Jacobin defenders of the administrative monarchy as republicans and the Girondin advocates of constitutional government as royalists. The fact that the Jacobins, as soon as they had consolidated their power and driven the invaders from France, assumed the Girondin crusade to rid their world of kings, in no way changed their basic orientation. Originally they had asked nothing more than that Louis become their Revolutionary king and had cheered him wildly when he donned a Phrygian cap in a balcony of the Tuileries. In fact, it was this instinctive commitment to the monarchical principle of the administrative state that made them so vindictive about his inadequacy and so intolerant of the Girondins' devotion to constitutional restraints on governmental action. It had been just such checks that had made it possible for the nobles to forestall desperately needed reforms for decades; and the Jacobins had no intention of allowing anything of the sort to be revived.

To consolidate their position in Paris, the Jacobins dispatched the principal Girondins; and to reassert the authority of the government in the provinces, they improvised a monstrous national administration by reinforcing the authority of the local clubs through the threat of mass executions. If by inducing sheer panic they succeeded in mobilizing the country for victory, they also provoked desperate resistance.

With the Republican armies suffering dangerous reverses in the field, separatist elements in a number of port cities took to arms. The Committee of Public Safety succeeded in suppressing the insurrection, but at the cost of sacking Caen, Bordeaux, and Lyon, and conducting mass reprisals in all affected areas, in the first civil war in France since the sixteenth century. Because this Federalist revolt against the Jacobin government was based mainly in port cities, it seems plausible that it represented the last stand of the old commercial society against integration in the administrative state. The subsequent history of these Federalists is hard to trace because only those who disappeared from view survived defeat and repression. Under the Jacobin Republic, capital wealth was at least as compromising as landed estates, and its records were easier to destroy. Merchants and bankers left little documentary evidence of their fortunes during this period; for men of wealth, bourgeois as well as noble, the Terror was a period to survive.

With the Girondins liquidated, the Federalists crushed, and the foreign invaders in rout, the Jacobins were not merely victorious on all fronts, they appeared unassailable. But men capable of such desperate action recognized few limits in success, and Robespierre and his followers tried to ride their political whirlwind to the ultimate moral reformation of the nation. As their standards of public virtue rose, so did the number of those in the Convention who saw themselves vulnerable to denunciation. Eventually these potential victims acted in self-defense and overturned their self-appointed prosecutors. Thermidor turned the tide of terror; and if the executions did not end before a number of prominent Jacobins had fallen victims of the reaction, the rank and file of the party survived as a numerous and indigenous provincial elite ready to help reconstitute the administrative state of the old agricultural society at the first opportunity.

Following the fall of Robespierre, still another constitution was drafted and another government established. Known as the Directory, after its corporate executive, this regime rapidly earned a reputation for corruption that neither time nor Crane Brinton have successfully dimmed. Nevertheless, it lasted four years—not a bad record for the period—and prepared the way for Napoleon's Consulate. Its electorate was limited by property qualifications, and its two representative assemblies were purged in successive minor coups. By eliminating extremists from both left and right, the government had so narrowed its political base that, when Bonaparte staged his *coup de Brumaire*, there was no popular resistance.

Although the Directors have traditionally been criticized for shortsighted cynicism, the fact is that they were not concerned with politics. Because no new administrative system had yet been created, they had little contact with the country; in any case, their business was quite simply the army. Having driven the foreign invaders from the soil of France, the Republican forces began to "liberate" the rest of Europe. Very quickly they demonstrated that this service to humanity could be made to pay. For some time, the proceeds of conquest supported the government, which in turn served as the purchasing office of the army. It was the Directors' shameless exploitation of military contracts that earned them their imperishable notoriety; but their scandalous behavior did not affect the public image of the army, which became enormously popular, not only for its victories, but for its implementation of the revolutionary commitment to careers open to talent.

Whether the Directors and their hangers-on represented the old commercial-financial community of the port cities has yet to be established, but they were unquestionably operating with large sums of capital and were regularly accused of favoring "commercial interests." In spite of their extravagant profits, however, they failed to put their new business on a firm foundation. Not recognizing that war and conquest cannot be made to pay indefinitely, they failed to re-establish any internal administrative-fiscal organization capable of supporting the state and its armies. Instead, they decided to strengthen their position against mounting political opposition by bringing a general into their organization. That they happened to pick Bonaparte was, in terms of their personal ambitions, a matter of poor judgment or bad luck; but that the army, in the person of one or another of its many able officers, should sooner or later have taken over this civilian office was all but inevitable.

Bonaparte began his rule with a vigorous campaign to restore law, order, and central administration throughout the country. The charge that public services, particularly the maintenance of roads, was all but nonexistent and brigandage rampant in pre-Brumaire France has generally been dismissed as Bonapartist apologetics; but given the history of the preceding decade, it is plausible. By the end of the Consulate, in any case, France was once again governed by a central bureaucracy that incorporated all the reforms demanded in the *cahiers*. With the Empire, Napoleon revived the monarchy in more than a ceremonial sense. He had re-established a thoroughly rationalized form of the old military-administrative structure on the fiscal base of the agricultural hinterland. He then proceeded to reorganize the economy of occupied Europe to favor that of France to the advantage of the peasants.

Napoleon was, as has often been remarked, the last and greatest of the enlightened despots. What has been conceded less often is that his regime was widely popular, at least until his military gambling brought defeat. It is even worth asking why the Continental System did not take root and integrate the rest of Europe in peace and prosperity with France. In spite of the inevitable aggravations of military occupation, the French had originally been welcomed as liberators; and their reforms had been jealously preserved in much of the territory through which they passed. Even if the local reactions did vary from area to area, the introduction of codified law, bureaucratic efficiency, and a certain degree of territorial amalgamation were unquestioningly accepted as benefits, especially in western Germany and northern Italy. To sweep aside existing socio-economic structures and integrate the local population into the fiscal economy of France, however, proved quite another matter. Not only did it threaten deeply rooted habits and vested interests, but it often contravened the laws of transport.

The Continental System had hurt the population of the occupied coasts quite as much as it had the English and had engendered hostility to the Empire of much the sort manifested by the port cities against the Bourbons. But if Napoleon's efforts to impose his system on all of Europe provoked resistance on the Continent that hastened his defeat, his ultimate enemy was England. It was fitting that he should have met his final downfall at her hands and in a battle for the Low Countries, the traditional European base of the Atlantic community. If England is viewed as the communications center of an oceanic commercial society, its stubborn efforts to defend the freedom of European ports becomes more understandable. In fact, the wars of the Coalitions can be seen as the final decisive campaigns of a great second Hundred Years' War, between the Atlantic community and the French for control of the Continent and its littoral. Given the advantages of the commercial society, its incomparable wealth, its enclaves of support along Europe's shores, and the mobility of its water-borne forces, the outcome of the struggle could hardly have been in doubt at any time. But with the development of the unprecedented economic power of the new industrial-commercial complex that the English were mounting during this last phase, as well as the virtually inexhaustible supply of allied armies that it could finance and frequently supply, not even a soldier of Napoleon's genius had a chance of ultimate victory. If he could have sealed his coasts, he might conceivably have made his Continental System work and even have succeeded in amalgamating the more backward and hostile sections of Europe. If he had, however, England would still have retained the unanswerable advantage of being at once immune to direct military attack and able to strike at will with contraband, subsidies, or naval force.

When Napoleon finally set sail for St. Helena, he left France shorn of its revolutionary conquests, but with its revolution fully implemented and secure. If he had failed to integrate the rest of Europe in the fiscal economy of his Continental System, he clearly believed, as was noted in the previous chapter, that he had finally united the disparate factions of French society into a single nation-state. Surely he was right, and Montlosier wrong, about the nobles. They lost their independent status in 1789, and their only future lay in the monarchy, their erstwhile rival. Furthermore, the great ports, having been cut off from the Atlantic by the wars, had obviously lost their place in the commercial community and appeared to have been absorbed in the Empire. This assimilation, however, was administrative, not economic. If the ports had not prospered under the blockade, they had survived by the self-generative economic power of cities, not by the development of inland commerce with the hinterland. Thus, even though they never recovered their old commercial importance after the War, they continued to exist and even prosper as independent capitalist enclaves, and gradually resumed their efforts to control the monarchy.

Under Napoleon, the old symbiotic relationship between capital wealth and the administrative state was resumed, and it was the bankers who arranged the Restoration after his abdication. Too little attention has been paid to the effortless character of the transition, essentially unmarred by the Hundred Days, from Empire to Restoration. The country accepted the Bourbons with the same ease that the Bourbons accepted the revolutionary settlement and, with it, the most powerful central government in the world. The essential change effected by the Restoration was to replace Napoleon and his consultative assemblies with Louis XVIII and two independent legislative chambers, one hereditary and the other elected by tightly restricted suffrage. Since all major titles were recognized, those of the Empire as well as of the old regime, the Chamber of Peers contained a majority of Napoleonic nobles; but since the electorate was limited to the largest taxpayers, the Chamber of Deputies was dominated by the old landed aristocrats. The peasants, who still constituted more than half of the population, neither received nor apparently expected any representation; the lesser bourgeois of the towns and cities, on the other hand, nurtured an increasingly bitter resentment at their disenfranchisement.

By and large, however, the transition was accomplished with such ease as to suggest that it was arranged by men with a lively sense of what would be acceptable to the vast majority of the population. If Talleyrand has generally been given credit for engineering Louis XVIII's return in order to avoid the reprisals he would have to expect from any other candidate, the requirements of the personal security of the Prince of Benevento should not be taken, as they so often have been, as sufficient explanation for the configuration of the new regime. Its institutions actually reflected the composition and interests of the elites who controlled the country. The two sovereign chambers unabashedly represented the great landowners, still predominantly surviving aristocrats from the *ancien régime* and the *notables* of the Empire: the great administrators, suppliers, and bankers who managed Napoleon's affairs at home while he was occupied abroad. Except for three important modifications, the Restoration was neither more nor less than a continuation of the Empire, with Napoleon himself replaced by an innocuous figure; the consultative assemblies transformed into tutelary chambers; and the army reduced below the level at which it could threaten France or Europe.

Even if the Charter can properly be described as a constitution, the regime it established was not a constitutional monarchy in the British sense. The government was still an administrative monarchy, but the monarch had been expanded into a collegiate body. The Chambers of the Restoration no more constituted a separate legislative branch, in Montesquieu's sense, than the executive and judicial *functions* of the English legislative government had represented independent powers, in his day. The real function of the new Chambers was to diffuse the enormous administrative power of the chief executive among the representatives of the country's elite, so that the regime could more accurately be called a corporate, than a constitutional, monarchy.

The period of the Restoration was surprisingly free of political issues. Even the confrontations that led to its dissolution in July 1830 were more the product of royal eccentricities than the conflict of substantial interests. Read superficially, the historical record suggests that Napoleon had been right in his boast that he had unified the French into a single, rational nation-state. The nobles, the traditional opponents of royal authority, emerged under Louis XVIII as the principal supporters of the throne, the most enthusiastic becoming *"plus royaliste que le roi."* And the merchant bankers of the port cities, having lost their entry to the Atlantic community, seemed also to have been assimilated by the monarchical society, although their transformation is more difficult to follow.

Whether Talleyrand and the consortium of Napoleonic *notables* he represented were in any sense direct heirs of the old commercial community need not be established here. Their support of the Restoration clearly was motivated by their involvement in the national debt; and like their predecessors in this role in the *ancien régime,* they were concerned with the fiscal administration of the state. They seem to have had no political interest of their own beyond protecting their investment, and there is no reason to suspect them of hostility to the regime, which they themselves had established. Indeed, their contribution to the fall of Charles X seems to have been intended to preserve the monarchy from the vagaries of an unreliable monarch. After all, the King had first been challenged in the Chamber of Deputies by his own aristocratic supporters who apparently feared that his flamboyant gestures might set off popular reactions; and it was only when Charles openly threatened them with a *coup d'état* that Talleyrand and his associates entered the struggle and unleashed the press and poster campaign that brought the Paris mob into the streets and sent the King abroad.

The entire little melodrama was played out on a barren political stage unencumbered by issues of substance. The law of sacrilege that established death by drawing and quartering as the penalty for disrupting religious services or processions was a shocker, but there was no more chance of its being applied than of the proposed law of primogeniture passing in the Chamber of Peers. Even the indemnification of the nobles by a reduction of interest on state bonds caused much less concern than has sometimes been assumed. In fact, the regime suffered far more literary abuse than serious political attack. The interests of the financial operators in Paris were quite different from those of the landed aristocrats, and the two do not seem to have been in conflict. When the crisis came, it was the bankers who had the presence of mind to have their own candidate installed on the vacant throne before any opposition could be mounted.

Although the July Monarchy has traditionally been treated as a separate regime, it was in most respects a continuation of the Restoration. The differences pointed to in textbooks were largely matters of style: Louis Philippe became the "king of the French" instead of "King of France"; the tricolor was restored; and Catholicism was slightly downgraded to the "religion of most Frenchmen." The most substantial modifications were the insertion of the adjective "responsible" before "ministry" in the Charter and the extension of the suffrage; but the significance of even these innovations could easily be exaggerated. The purpose of their authors seems to have been, first, to establish the corporation's better control over their "monarch," and second, to broaden their political base; but there was considerable confusion about the meaning of "responsible ministry," and the expansion of the electorate from 90,000 to 300,000 out of an adult male population of over six million seems insignificant. Actually the July Monarchy was intended merely to establish the hegemony of those Orleanist oligarchs whom Beau de Loménie has identified as covert bourgeois traitors to the monarchy and enemies of his true France.

Because it was followed, rather than preceded, by proletarian action, class-struggle historians have difficulty with the Revolution of 1830. This apparent anomaly can be explained by two separate factors. First, the economic changes that were responsible for the mounting social tensions that would reach a climax in the June Days of 1848 only began with the end of the Napoleonic wars; and second, they affected the growing provincial cities of the hinterland as much, if not more, than Paris and the great ports. The population of France is generally estimated to have been about twenty-five million in 1789, and the first official census in 1801 placed it at something over twenty-eight million. Subsequent figures show a fairly constant but, compared to most other European countries, modest rate of growth, so that on the eve of 1914 the population was approaching forty million. But these apparently innocuous statistics hide a far more radical development. Because the peasant population, having saturated the subsistence economy, remained virtually constant throughout the period, the increase was channeled into the cities, which pushed the urban population from some three million in 1789 to six million in 1801, to twelve million in mid-century, and to twenty million at the outbreak of World War I.

Urban growth was already causing problems in the eighteenth century. While the port cities lived by their own water-borne commerce, those of the hinterland had to depend on the resources of their immediate environs and, as a result, were difficult to feed. Contemporary social commentators speculated that, without unlimited access to water transport, it would not be possible to provision cities of more than a few hundred thousand inhabitants. Few actually approached this order of magnitude; but in spite of the obvious and apparently insuperable problems of supply, inland cities continued to grow at a rapid rate in the first half of the nineteenth century before the transportation revolution could have altered their basic economic structure. The early nineteenth century was not a period in which new towns, as in the seventeenth, or cities, as in the late nineteenth, were formed. Instead, the old ones grew, with the larger growing faster. The largest, to be sure, were Paris and the peripheral cities that could, with one or two partial exceptions, be easily supplied by water. The next category in size were the provincial capitals, which, although usually located on some river or stream, were seldom ports in any meaningful sense. Even so, they too continued to expand, as did their small counterparts, the new *chefs lieu* of the rural departments.

Few, if any, of these inland cities owed their continued expansion to large-scale industry or widespread commerce. Virtually all had begun as governmental centers, either for some feudal lord or the monarchy, and had changed little before the Restoration. For lack of any obvious explanation of the general growth of these essentially self-contained inland cities, it seems necessary to consider the possibility that urban agglomerations, once they exceed some undetermined size, develop self-generative tendencies or powers. What the critical mass is need not detain us here, except to note that it was clearly more than the "2,000" used to define "urban" in French statistics. Throughout the nineteenth century, towns of a few thousand tended to remain, as they had begun, local points of agricultural exchange, necessary and wholly integrated elements of the subsistence-agricultural society—not so their larger neighbors.

In contrast to the market towns, the small cities of the interior operated their own usually self-contained, but monetary economies. Because their inhabitants had become highly differentiated and specialized, they could produce more goods and services per capita than their counterparts in the smaller market towns. But because they had to procure the bulk of their food from their immediate environs, and their populations were too large to merge in the subsistence economy of the hinterland, they were forced, sooner or later, to absorb the adjacent farms into their own commercial communities. These lands were then turned into grain plantations, or other commercial exploitations, by the "rural bourgeoisie," who have caused historians so much semantic anguish. It was they who managed to supply the local urban markets with the food that enabled them to develop into self-sufficient, dynamic economic units, growing within but independent of the old subsistence society.

Population estimates and figures show, moreover, that these provincial cities, while statistically insignificant in the pre-Revolutionary monarchy, had become an important segment of the nation under the Restoration. With the general increase in the size of urban units went a progressive increase in their commercial activity; and with the end of the Napoleonic wars and the collapse of the Continental System, their development was destined to be affected by renewed contact with the Atlantic community. During almost exactly the same years that the French were working out their own political salvation, the English were mounting their industrial revolution. Not only did the Revolutionary wars present England with a virtual monopoly of oceanic commerce, but her new industry produced an unlimited supply of cheap consumer goods to dump on its markets at prices that at once made competition impossible and still earned enormous profits. To protect this unprecedented situation, the English attempted to prevent the export of their new industrial techniques and machines; but (as the United States was to learn with its atomic monopoly a century and a half later) they found their efforts to maintain technical secrets as unavailing as they were naïve. Moreover, they discovered that there were even greater profits in the sale of capital equipment and that its export would have less effect on their already established markets than they had feared.

In France, the flood of goods coming from the English Midlands could not be sold at their original low prices, except in cities accessible to water transport. Cheap transportation was at least as important to the manufacture and marketing of cheap goods as cheap power. Until the French developed inexpensive inland transport, they would not constitute a mass market for industrial products, either foreign or domestic. But well before they achieved that transformation, the growing urban markets of the hinterland had begun importing English equipment for the mechanization of their own local industries; and during the first half of the nineteenth century, the cities of the French interior were better markets for English machinery than English goods. Expensive as it was to move a steam engine or power loom inland, it was a single operation and could be managed far more easily than the constant flow of large quantities of cheap textiles. Economic histories record the sudden appearance of steam engines and small mills throughout the provinces at just this time; yet for all the importance of this shift from hand or water power to steam, it should be noticed that this development reinforced, rather than revolutionized, existing economic patterns. Even if local industries may have extended their market radii slightly, they did not produce highly specialized products for wide distribution in the manner of Manchester or Birmingham. In France, the introduction of power machinery came as the ultimate phase of the old local economies, not the first step toward mass industrialization.

This is not to say, however, that mechanization had no impact on existing social and political structures. Not only did it contribute to the continuing growth of the provincial cities, but it transformed them from primarily administrative centers into capitalist communities. Moreover, although there was little exchange of goods from city to city, a sense of common interest began to develop among the new entrepreneurs during the July Monarchy. Living cells of a new urban capitalist society were not only proliferating throughout France but were putting out tentacles of communication that would later develop into a cohesive system. This process may have been initiated by the port cities, which not only expedited English machinery into the interior but quite possibly provided the capital for its purchase, transportation, and installation as well. From 1830 on, however, another unifying factor is clearly evident. Even though the emerging capitalist society was pre-industrial, in the full sense, it created local factory proletariats and with them a brutal if widely dispersed class struggle, which, with a morbid irony, unified the new entrepreneurial class in the political defense of its privileges and property.

Emmanuel Beau de Loménie based his analysis on the assumption that the *grands bourgeois* were forced by their investment in the railroads to concentrate on controlling the state, which not only guaranteed the interest on the bonds but had the right to acquire the lines. Without questioning the importance of this insight, it now seems necessary to add that, by the very early 1830's, the new provincial capitalist bourgeois, by no means all *grands*, were already dependent on the state for police protection and, therefore, were directly involved in politics.

Whatever class exploitation was built into the agricultural society, its basic purpose was to provide subsistence for its population, which meant that—except for famine situations— the direct threat of starvation for even its poorest members was rare. In the new capitalist communities, however, the chief product was not food, but money. Originally the labor force for the early factories seems to have been drawn from the agricultural society on a seasonal basis, by offering marginal employment to peasants who retained their subsistence base. Under these circumstances, miserable as they were, factory wages attracted workers from the nonmonetary peasant society; and as long as they remained supplementary, these earnings probably represented a net gain for the recipients. But with the steady expansion of the population, the rural society became saturated; and its surplus labor force was forced into the cities, converting the quasi-peasants into a full-time factory proletariat. This meant, first, that they bought all their food for cash at urban prices; and that as a result, their wages dwindled to a dangerous minimum. Their employers, moreover, had no concept of responsibility for their support. In their own capitalist terms, they viewed labor as a commodity, which, like any other, they could buy or ignore. Because the adjustment of the new factory production to local demands was awkward, these entrepreneurs found it to their financial advantage to run their plants intermittently, leaving their workers in a desperately precarious situation. Unemployment meant starvation, and the class struggle developed as an integral part of the mechanization of the local urban economies.

The class struggle, it should be noted, did not separate capitalist mill owners from their proletarian workers but locked them in a hostile relationship from which there was no escape for either. The workers, that is, were forced migrants to the cities who not only could not return to the agricultural society but would be followed by more like themselves. The entrepreneurs, on the other hand, had committed their capital to mills that could be run at a profit only with a cheap and flexible supply of labor. Together they were condemned to create, within the growing cities of the interior as well as the periphery, a new capitalist society that would become the "other France."

CHAPTER SIX

The Schizophrenic Nation

———•———

To MOST HISTORIANS, the emergence of modern industry in France during the first half of the nineteenth century has implied the simultaneous development of a capitalist economy and the class struggle. That the new industry was producing a new proletariat is easy to demonstrate; that class interests dominated French politics is not. Marx himself recognized that it was the behavior of the peasants that muddied his class analysis; but neither his explanation that they had been corrupted by the parceling of land and the taste for property it engendered nor his obvious assumption that they were stupid could salvage his thesis. Given his background and his preoccupation with the English industrial model, it is perhaps not surprising that Marx failed to recognize the existence and persistence of an independent agricultural society. Lenin, at least instinctively, had a better understanding of peasants and saved his Revolution by accepting their aberrations and promising them the land. As his successors could testify, however, this gesture did not transform the peasants into an instant proletariat. Even if the events of 1917 in Russia, or of 1789 in France, seem to bear out Marx's conviction that peasants without land would be far more radical than those who, like the French of 1848, had a little, these examples do not prove that landless peasants could be recruited directly into the workers' cause. Nor were the true rural landowners capitalists any more than their peasants were proletarians. They belonged to different societies, each with its own discrete economy and each instinctively inclined to resist the encroachment of the new capitalism on their way of life. Indeed, it was the dynamic character of the new capitalist economy that caused both the trouble and the confusion in French politics in the last century and a half.

The dependence of modern industrial societies on accelerating growth for their economic health has been too long a truism to require elaboration here. What has been much less widely recognized, however, is the essentially static nature of the traditional agricultural societies. This statement should not be read as a claim that French peasant life underwent no modifications or that its agriculture failed to increase its production, but rather that the population of rural France remained virtually constant and that its orientation continued to be subsistence farming during the century following the Revolution, a period in which the urban population and its industrial production were both growing steadily. Because, at least initially, the cities were largely self-sufficient, self-generating units providing their own market for their own production and even feeding themselves from adjacent plantation (capitalist) farms, they might have grown within the agricultural society without coming into serious conflict with it.

Two developments of the mid-nineteenth century, however, were to render this coexistence by mutual indifference increasingly difficult. The first was the reintroduction of universal suffrage in 1848, and the second was the building of a national system of railroads beginning in the 1850's. The impact of each of these revolutionary new departures will need to be examined in the context of French history, but it might be noted that together they forced the two societies to cohabit not merely a single territory, but a single political-administrative state. If day-to-day political issues tended to develop within each, rather than between the two communities, universal suffrage meant that no single class within either was likely to be able to muster a majority of the combined bodies politic and, therefore, that a threatened minority in either could, and very rapidly would, seek electoral allies in the other. To understand how this practice evolved and worked it is necessary to re-examine the history of the period.

It was fitting, if coincidental, that the new capitalist community emerged under the *régime censitaire* of the July Monarchy. Even if the bankers, who placed their colleague, Louis Philippe, on the throne, were not yet deeply involved in the new society by 1830, the rising provincial entrepreneurs were. But if these latter sensed their affinity with the regime and appear to have supported it from the outset, so did an important number of the landed aristocrats. Indeed, it is still difficult to analyze political alignments of this period in modern terms. For one thing, politics played a very much smaller, although increasing, role in the life of France than they do today. By and large, the peasants asked little of the state except that it function effectively; and they still accounted for over half the population. Political interest seems to have been limited to confrontations between the larger landowners and the professional bourgeoisie of the country towns on the one hand, and that of the entrepreneurs and the urban proletariat on the other. Under the Restoration, less than two percent of the country's adult males had exercised the vote, and they were seldom involved with serious political issues.

With the July Monarchy and the trebling of the electorate, to some five percent, this changed, but the reasons for the change are not entirely clear. Obviously, in extending the suffrage, the Orleanists intended to improve their weak electoral position in relation to their more numerous rivals, the aristocratic landowners. There is, however, no reason to assume that they intended to draw the necessary support from the new provincial capitalists. Rather, they probably hoped to attract small-town Jacobins by opening to them the possibility of political careers. The bourgeois style of the monarchy, with the return to the tricolor as a symbol, seems to have been a bid for the support of this group. The cartoonists and satirists of the time played on this theme with devastating sketches of threadbare deputies making their way to Paris on a bony nag, to return home in finery and a carriage. The older histories of the reign also confirm this view in their insistence on Guizot's exploitation of the situation by providing the needy deputies with government jobs in return for their parliamentary votes.

Some recent studies have challenged this tradition, with evidence that most of the deputies were men of substance, among whom only a few were really dependent on the minister's largess, and that an easy majority would have supported the regime in any case. While true in a technical sense, this contention is potentially misleading. By definition, the voters and their deputies were men of property and as such would tend, other things being equal, to favor the *status quo*. But, in comparison with the preceding regime, the electorate of the July Monarchy was much less wealthy. Those belonging to the richest one and a half percent of the population could easily afford to serve their government without remuneration; those of the next three and a half percent quite possibly could not. Moreover, they would include many of the small-town bourgeois, who were direct heirs of the Jacobins. As such, they would tend to oppose the regime as much for its financial as monarchical character. In addition, unless attached to it by some immediate personal interest, they would instinctively look forward to the second coming of the Republic, not only as an ideological liberation from both royal and capitalist "oppression," but as an opening to new careers in the service or government of the state. In the meantime, they lived with the *régime censitaire* without too much difficulty. They served the purposes of the oligarchs by balancing the votes of the Legitimists in the rural districts, for which they were rewarded with an occasional seat as deputy; at best this was *mariage de convenance*.

During its early years, the July Monarchy was occupied with labor problems. Only diligent and frequently harsh suppression kept the new factory workers from organizing and striking to improve their miserable and precarious situation. For these efforts, however, they found no support among the limited electorate, and their plight did not become a political issue. By the end of the 1830's they had been effectively, if temporarily, subdued; and the regime found itself contending with another problem, the challenge of the railroads. From the first appearance of this invention in England, it had been only a question of time before it would be exported to the Continent. A few small experimental lines were already in operation in France by 1840, when the directors of the regime began the technical planning and political maneuvering necessary for the construction of a national system.

This undertaking was bound to bring the state into the economic affairs of the country to an unprecedented degree and, as a result, to involve more and more of the population in politics.

The French money market was currently suffering from a glut of capital due to the mounting profits from the new provincial industries, and one of the chief motivating forces behind the railroad boom was the search for new investments. The total operation was so enormous, however, that the country's bankers could not begin to underwrite it alone. Even though they might have been content to continue building local lines to serve local purposes, they were inevitably caught up in the political debate and financial speculation set off by the announcement of a national plan. Although little actual construction was accomplished in the 1840's, legislation was passed that projected a national system of five great lines radiating from Paris. The state undertook to build the roadbeds and guarantee interest on private capital invested in equipping and operating the lines. The extraordinary scale of the venture and its predictable profits almost immediately transformed the railroad bonds into the principal outlet for available capital. It was this opportunity for investment, in conjunction with the role of the state in the development and control of the enterprise, that brought the *grands bourgeois*, as Beau de Loménie has so persuasively argued, to concern themselves with the political defense of their committed fortunes.

Under the July Monarchy, however, the impact of the railroads was still indirect, producing a general fever of speculation that reached even small investors in the provinces, such as the new entrepreneurs, and a bitter struggle among the major bankers for shares (that is, bonds) in the most promising lines. Both contributed to the collapse of the regime in 1848, but the stage was set by the catastrophic crop failure of 1846. Although France suffered less than many parts of Europe from that disaster, food prices rose dangerously and remained inflated into 1848. At about the same time, the railroad boom produced a hectic prosperity, especially in Paris, where paper fortunes were made and spent at an increasing tempo. As a result, the city's artisans, builders, cabinetmakers, tailors, and all the rest of the luxury tradesmen were extended to their limits. With the inevitable break in the bond market, the orders for luxuries ceased overnight, throwing large numbers of laborers out of work, while food was still in short supply.

To compound the situation, a number of disgruntled leaders of the regime began to mount a campaign for electoral reform, apparently in an effort to break the King's hold on the majority in the Chamber, which Guizot orchestrated through various forms of official manipulation and corruption. Behind this cynical pretense of constitutional government, Louis Philippe was exercising arbitrary control of state business, particularly the allotment of railroad bonds to his own personal profit. Exactly what provoked the final crisis is difficult to determine, but there is evidence that the King's disillusioned colleagues, aware that they were being cheated out of a fair share of the railroad bonanza, decided to act in self-defense. Pulling the old script of 1830 from their files, they unleashed an inflammatory attack on the regime in the Paris press, only to discover that the mob they had let loose this time was twice as large and far more ugly than the last and quite beyond their power to contain.

When it came, the Revolution was not the result of a confrontation between the incumbent regime and a widespread and well-organized opposition, but rather an explosion of diverse and desperate frustrations. While it is certainly possible to see cleavages in the confusion, the fundamental struggle seems to have been between the old agricultural and the new urban social systems. The Paris mob that forced the King to fly and the provisional government to proclaim the Republic and the Right to Work was largely made up of "workers," and some of its leaders were social revolutionaries. As a result, historians have tended to see 1848 as a class confrontation; but all evidence suggests that the model for this new Republic was the First (that is, a Parisian), Jacobin, rural, and administrative regime. If the founders of the Second were anti-monarchical by doctrine, they were also anti-parliamentary, and had opposed the July Monarchy as much for its financial orientation and parliamentary corruption as for its throne. They were, of course, instinctively anti-capitalist, but it should be emphasized that they had neither understanding of, nor sympathy for, the new industrial proletariat. In 1793 and 1794, their predecessors had used the urban mobs against the Federalist bourgeois of the peripheral cities. In 1848, these latter-day Jacobins apparently hoped to mobilize support among the workers against their common capitalist opponents, but they had no intention of turning them against the established social order. Although this position made good sense in the context of the rural republic, it produced deception and disillusion among the exploited classes of the new urban society; and the consequent confusion has been transferred from the politics of the day to most subsequent historical accounts.

The character and behavior of the Paris mob during the Revolution illustrates the point. Although Karl Marx called Paris the proletarian city *par excellence*, it may have had a smaller percent of industrial workers than any other important urban center in France. Probably not more than a tenth of the capital's "proletariat" were factory workers. The rest, not counting the subproletariat of porters and assorted riffraff, were craftsmen or tradesmen and their apprentices or journeymen, most of whom were as instinctively attached to property as any peasants.

Following a period of near famine, shortages, and sudden, general unemployment, the Right to Work appealed to these urban Jacobins as an obligation the state owed its citizens in a crisis, but not as the first step toward social revolution. The practical translation of this right into the hastily improvised National Workshops markedly altered the situation in the Capital. Amounting to nothing more than an open-ended government work-relief program, intended to absorb the local mob, this institution offered a daily pittance to any worker who appeared. As a result, the unemployed factory hands from the provincial cities flocked to Paris and not only doubled the size of the mob, but injected a new revolutionary potential into the already critical situation.

Behind the confused struggles that occupied the Provisional Government and the Paris population during the spring of 1848, a more or less conscious contest developed between Jacobin leaders and representatives of the fallen regime for constitutional position and political power. In spite of its very limited base in the total population, the July Monarchy had staffed the government for eighteen years, with the result that a majority of the political and administrative elite in Paris were its supporters. These included not only the higher government officials and most of the established political figures; but—because of the continuing threat of the Revolution—many of the lesser administrators and petty bourgeois, who in spite of their republican inclinations rallied to ex-Orleanist leaders. At the same time, with Louis Philippe in ignominous exile and his regime utterly discredited, most Orleanists found it convenient to become "moderate" republicans. Obviously, some Parisians were more "republican" than others. In this disguise, the Orleanists attempted to re-establish their corporate rule through the new assemblies, first the Constituent and then the Legislative; and they were at least partially successful in establishing the superior "republican" virtue of representative government over either direct popular action or presidential rule. If they were not able to translate this ideological victory into political power, they did succeed in confusing political terminology both then and since.

In 1848 there was nothing parliamentary in the republican tradition. And what almost no one, except the new capitalist bourgeoisie, wanted in 1848 was more of the corruption and financial manipulation associated with the Orleanists' regime. Moreover, whatever one may think of mob rule, it had unimpeachable "republican" credentials in France, and a reasonable precedent for presidential rule could easily be found in the plebiscitary regime of the First Consul. Not only the Jacobins of 1848, but most citizens of rural France, were disillusioned with parliamentary government; and the denouement of the Republic in the *coup d'état* was no mere irony of history. The standard class analyses of this period—today the standard analyses are more or less "class"-oriented—make much of the innate conservatism of the French bourgeois and, at least by implication, blame the Empire on their "cynical" resort to universal suffrage to bring the peasants into the electoral balance.

This traditional approach misses a number of important points. First, since the Provisional Government did not dare exclude the mass of urban citizens from elections in 1848, there was no ground for discriminating against the rural population; universal suffrage was not introduced as a political maneuver, but as a practical necessity. Second, although the peasants had obviously lost their revolutionary fervor of 1793, they did not all vote for reactionary candidates. To understand the conservatism of the time, it is essential to recognize that virtually all of agricultural France, from the small-town republicans through the peasants to the landed aristocrats, believed in the sanctity of property. Moreover, the majority saw the new capitalist economy as an insidious threat to their own rural society. The differences between them hinged on their attitude toward the new urban lower classes. If to most aristocrats and peasants these factory workers represented an extreme social threat, to many radicals they looked like potential republican converts and voters. After all, they too were victims of the capitalist regime and presumably only needed to be rescued to become good Jacobins; but this interest should not be construed as sympathy for proletarian revolution.

The violent class confrontation in Paris in 1848 was due to this misunderstanding compounded by miscalculation and mismanagement. With the mob in control of the Capital at the end of February and the Right to Work established, the National Workshops did seem to offer a way to get the unemployed off the streets. The bourgeois were frightened and helpless, but the radicals thought they saw a political opportunity. Neither, however, seems to have anticipated the convergence on the Capital of the hordes of provincials who rapidly doubled the Workshop contingents. The resulting situation was intolerable. Not only was the cost of the pittance wages driving the government to the brink of bankruptcy; but the influx from the provinces continued increasing the revolutionary potential day by day. The one possible hope of avoiding a catastrophe was to get these immigrants out of the city before all available funds evaporated. In May it was announced that members of the Workshops would be given the option of returning home, with a small severance wage, or of being mobilized into the army.

The motives behind, and implications of, this maneuver were

transparent to those against whom it was directed. In addition to dispersing the provincial workers, it would halve the Paris mob, reducing it to manageable proportions. Reading their intended fate without illusion the two groups—or more accurately, the militants of both—made common cause and prepared to resist. By now confident of its military strength, the government first withdrew its forces from the city, to allow the rebels to concentrate, and then returned to the attack. The ensuing June Days may have been the most savage outburst of class war in the nineteenth century.

While the "proletarian" character of the resistance is generally recognized, historians do not agree about either its origin or significance, particularly in relation to the Commune of 1871. Why, for example, should this latter insurrection, for all its militancy, have posed so much less social threat? Any answer to this historically embarrassing question will be speculative at best. Such evidence as we have, however, suggests that the indigenous Paris mob, in 1871, was still composed essentially of the same petty tradesmen, artisans and journeymen that had constituted the *"sans-culotte"* in 1793. In 1848, however, the numbers involved were much larger, and their "alienation," in the Marxian sense, may have been greater, particularly among the mass of unskilled laborers in the building trades, most of whom were probably recent arrivals from the provinces. The majority of the city's workers, however, were anything but social revolutionaries; and the *garde mobile*, who were particularly savage in repressing the rebels, were mostly of working-class origin.

It was the influx from the provinces that gave 1848 its special character. Not only was this the only significant march on Paris of the century; but in 1871, the Capital was sealed off from the country. The obvious implication that the revolutionary incentive came not from Paris, but the provinces, is exactly what this analysis should lead us to expect. The new factory industry had sprung up, during the past quarter century, in the small, local enterprises of the provincial cities; and the workers had been ruthlessly exploited from the start. In the 1830's they had made desperate efforts to defend themselves and had been brutally

suppressed. As a result, they would have been particularly vulnerable to the crisis of the late 1840's and accordingly responsive
to the relief offered in Paris. While they were surely not the only
immigrants to the Capital, these provincial factory workers provided the revolutionary impact that produced the June Days.

If the Revolution of 1848 began as the revolt of urban
masses against an inefficient, corrupt, and oligarchical regime, it
ended in the reassertion by the rural community of its preponderant position in the country. Naturally, if not quite inevitably, this took the form of the resurrection of the Republic
and, through it, of a revival of the Empire, all according to
Jacobin tradition. Once again France was ruled by its administrative state in the name of the entire people—and with their
overwhelming support—as all electoral consultations would
demonstrate right down to the end of the Empire.

The inherent conservatism of mid-century France was based
solidly in its agricultural community, which still outnumbered
the developing urban society by more than two to one. The new
proletariat, consisting of at most a million real factory workers,
was not yet politically effective in the cities, let alone the country at large. All of this puts the success of Louis Napoleon in a
different light than that in which it is usually presented. Granted
that among the candidates he, or at least his name, was probably
the only one known to the peasants, and that they provided
the solid base of his electoral victories, he was also accepted
from the very start by many of the Jacobins. In other words, he was
not the mere beneficiary of a rustic or panic vote but the obvious candidate of the rural-republican tradition. If Legitimists
supported him, it was undoubtedly in the belief that he would
maintain law and order, but also in the hope that he could keep
the Orleanists in their place. A. J. Tudesq, in his *Grands notables
en France,* has remarked on the occasional tendency of landed
aristocrats to support radical candidates against Orleanists during
the 1840's in an impromptu alliance he calls *"Carlo-républicaine."*

Actually, nothing could have been more logical or fitting
than that the first president of this Second Republic was not only
a nephew of the Bonaparte who had subverted the First Re-

public, but that he was on public record as determined to follow that illustrious example. The only irony in the situation derived from the efforts of Orleanists to use the unicameral National Assembly as a parliamentary check on the power of the new executive. This Republic, like its predecessor, was administrative rather than political, and anti-monarchical only in a formal sense. Instead of entrusting control of the administrative state to a "corporate" sovereign representing either landed or capital wealth, it assigned that authority to a president elected by universal suffrage. The Republic's devotees had been permanently turned against kings by Louis XVI's treason, but in any institutional sense they remained good monarchists at heart. Surprisingly few had any problem accepting either the First or Second Empire. The majority wanted a rationally and efficiently run country with careers available in the army or the state. For these purposes, an emperor was more effective than a constitutional monarch; and a plebescite provided a better base than a parliament.

The opposition that Louis Napoleon encountered in the Assembly while he was President seems to have been far more parliamentary than popular in origin. When elections were called in 1848, there was little time to identify candidates and develop campaigns. As a result, most deputies elected were local *notables* already known to the voters. Moreover, with the principal issue law and order, Legitimist landowners or Orleanist businessmen tended to run better in the conservative circumscriptions than the small-town Jacobins in spite of, rather than because of, their monarchist or parliamentary leanings. This meant that when they challenged Bonaparte's authority, these members of the Assembly were not necessarily reflecting the views of their constituents. The all but insuperable advantage enjoyed by such *notables* in electoral contests was to plague French politics well into the Third Republic, frequently putting representatives of narrow interests in power and thereby contributing to the widespread unpopularity of the government.

At the time of the *coup d'état* in 1851, as the subsequent plebiscite was to demonstrate, Napoleon had the overwhelming support of the country. Unconstitutional and even criminal as his seizure of power undoubtedly was, it did not, as has often been alleged, subvert the will of the people. Even most of the Orleanist opposition was at least partly won over by the protection he offered against the proletariat and the financial concessions he seemed prepared to make. Although much has, quite properly, been made of Louis Napoleon's St.-Simonian connections, these should not be allowed to obscure the fact that his principal commitment was to his own position and power. If, as he claimed, he understood the French better than the politicians, it was as an outsider who was not caught up in indigenous interests. Having lived most of his life in exile, he could view France with less passion and more perspective and then come to terms with the realities he perceived. The latter included not only the preponderance of the agricultural society within the country and his dependence on its support for the fulfillment of his ambitions but his need for a *modus vivendi* with the new capitalist society, as well.

Albert Guérard's characterization of Napoleon III as a "St.-Simon on horseback" who modernized France for the benefit of the people and against the selfish opposition of the capitalists is at least as misleading as it is intriguing. Uneasy as Napoleon undoubtedly made the financial elite, he did not do them serious harm, because he did not change the country's economy nearly so much as Guérard supposed. The chief unfinished business of the July Monarchy, when it was so rudely interrupted by the February riots, had been the railroads. Even if the legislation making their development safe for the banking interests was enacted, few actual lines were in operation; and those that were served local purposes. To the revolutionaries of 1848 this situation was a scandal, and one of the standard radical objectives was to nationalize the railroads. By building them, instead, Napoleon managed to take the steam out of the radical campaign without taking the bonds away from the bankers.

The task of completing the main rail system was one that suited Napoleon's St.-Simonian inclinations perfectly. Nothing, except perhaps interoceanic canals, would better serve the cause of international commerce, and therefore peace, than railroads. Further, the St.-Simonians believed in using the state as an instrument to remodel society according to their designs. In this they carried on the tradition of the great intendants of the *ancien régime* and established precedents for the planners and nationalizers of the mid-twentieth century. It is, therefore, interesting to examine the impact of their achievements and policies on France: first, in building the railroads and eventually the Suez canal, and second, the establishment of free trade. That the completion of the rail system contributed significantly to the immediate prosperity and long-range economic development of the country is beyond question; but the common assumption that this can be equated with the modernization, or specifically industrialization, of the French economy requires re-examination.

The building of the roadbeds was a vast undertaking, carried out by the government's famous department of *Ponts et chausées*. This meant not only an important expansion of the bureaucracy, but the mounting of a vast public-works program which stimulated business in every area it touched. At the same time, since most of the equipment was originally imported from England, the program produced relatively little concurrent expansion of industry in France. Even if some new iron works were built, notably in the region of Le Creusot and St. Etienne, and iron production continued to increase throughout the reign, it is important to remember that it was a full decade after Sedan before the country's first major base of heavy industry was created along the northeastern frontier. Much the same can be said about the manufacture of consumer goods. Although the railroads contributed to the growth of a national textile industry in the Lille area, they did not turn it into an English midlands, nor did they put all of the old local mills out of business.

The pattern of the rail network, taken together with the free-trade policy introduced by the Cobden-Chevalier Treaty in 1860, goes a long way toward explaining this surprisingly limited effect. The five great lines not only radiated from Paris, but in every case to the nation's great ports. The *Nord* went to the Channel, the *Ouest* to Nantes, the *Sud-ouest* to Bordeaux, the *P.L.M.* to Marseille, and the *Est* to Strasbourg and the Rhine. As a result, they facilitated foreign imports more than they stimulated domestic manufacture. It is perhaps surprising that they did not wipe out the indigenous industries of the provinces, but until the so-called "second" and "third networks" of feeder lines were completed under the Third Republic, much of the hinterland remained in semi-isolation. The peasant population, for example, showed no sign of decline, thereby indicating it was still continuing its essentially subsistence existence within the traditional agricultural society. Similarly, provincial entrepreneurs tended to survive; but they were in no position to attempt, as some critics claim they should have, to meet the challenge of foreign competition by expanding their own production and lowering their prices. They had neither the market, the resources, nor the capital to develop productive capacity even remotely comparable to that of England.

It is hardly surprising, given Paris' position at the center of the system, that it was the Capital, itself, that was transformed by the railroads. Already the largest city on the Continent, it suddenly exploded beyond recognition in size, wealth, and power. Not only was the old problem of food supply exorcised; but the rails provided a new accessibility, making it at once far easier for provincials to reach Paris and for the government to communicate with the provinces. The result was to accelerate the already irresistible centripetal force of bureaucratic administration. In its first phase, that is, the transportation revolution did more to modernize the old administrative state than to develop the new capitalist community. During this period the urban population continued to grow at an accelerating rate, with the larger cities growing faster and Paris fastest of all. The expansion of state services produced a new class of bourgeois *fonctionnaires*, particularly in the Capital. Given the role of Paris in the Empire, it was fitting, if not inevitable, that Napoleon should pour so much of his new administrative wealth and power into the reconstruction of the city. But behind the splendid new façades of the Capital, the hinterland continued its established way of life with surprisingly little change.

As Napoleon III approached the end of his reign, the two societies were reinforced in their mutual isolation and independence. The administrative state, reinvigorated by Imperial rule, was securely in control, not only of the agricultural community but of the entire country as well. At the same time, the urban-capitalist society had continued to grow and, in general, to prosper. What should be noted, however, is that it also was becoming increasingly aware of, and restive about, the government's authority. The bankers lived with the threat of nationalization of the railroads, the manufacturers suffered from the Empire's free trade, and the workers from its police. As a result, all elements of the capitalist community were concerned about the power of the state and the impending succession to its control.

Much has been made of the mounting republican opposition during the waning years of the Empire, but this highly vocal criticism seems to have come largely from ambitious young men who were at least as interested in place as principles. Certainly these neo-Jacobins, for all their denunciation of the Emperor's disastrous foreign policy, did nothing to help him avoid the debacle of 1870. Napoleon, however, was in no real danger from political opponents, because in spite of some decline, his electoral support remained solid throughout his reign. The most serious threat to the regime, at least after Bismarck, was the lack of an acceptable heir or successor. The Emperor, recognizing that his son was too young and weak to rule and his wife too irresponsible and unpopular to serve as regent, attempted to save the appearance of Empire by returning the reality of power to the oligarchy from which he had seized it. In the *Senatus Consultum* of March 1870, he re-established the constitutional monarchy by creating an independent parliament and making the ministry responsible to it. Because of the Prussian War, this new regime never had a chance to take root and has been generally ignored by historians; it did, however, set the pattern of government to which the Third Republic would return.

Before turning to the Third Republic, however, it is necessary to consider the fall of the Empire and the transition between the regime and its successor. Following the news of the Emperor's defeat and capture at Sedan, the Paris mob stormed the Hôtel de Ville on September 4, 1870, to proclaim the Jacobin Republic and seize control of the administrative state. If the Government of National Defense lacked the *audace* and failed to match the military successes of the First Republic, it never-

theless was intended to follow the Jacobins' example. Gambetta
escaped from beleaguered Paris to organize provincial armies;
but by the end of January, these were crushed and the Capital
starved into capitulation. By the terms of the armistice, arranged
by self-appointed and Orleanist emissaries, the Germans allowed the French to hold elections for a National Assembly that
would be competent to decide between continued resistance and
acceptance of the proffered treaty terms.

Because the national vote went heavily in favor of peace,
the large majority of the delegates elected were conservative:
half Legitimists and half Orleanists. In the social context of the
time, only men of some education and self-assurance could effectively stand as candidates, in the country bailiwicks at least,
which meant either the landed gentry, who stood for peace, or
the small-town professionals, who as radical republicans and
socialists had campaigned for rejection of the German terms and
the resumption of resistance. Similarly, in urban districts it was
the conservative peace candidates, usually leftover Orleanists,
who opposed the War. Thus, when the Assembly convened, not
only did it have an overwhelming mandate to conclude peace
but a large majority of monarchist members.

Given the circumstances, the deputies obviously represented
little but themselves, except on those specific issues of peace and
order on which they had been elected. Even if the "propertied"
classes from which they came had grown since the days of the
July Monarchy, they still constituted only a small percent of the
male population; and behind this façade of *notables* lay the
vast unorganized and essentially inexperienced electorate, which
contained a large majority of peasants and a growing minority of
urban proletarians. In this election, unlike the crisis of 1792, the
peasants did not feel that their interests (that is, property) were
as seriously threatened by the invaders as by continued resistance,
and, therefore, failed to respond to the *tocsins* of the Jacobins
and Paris. Instead, they voted for peace candidates, who were
frequently Legitimists.

In Paris, radical elements responded to the "monarchist"
election, the acceptance of the Treaty, and the humiliation of a
German victory parade in the Capital by preparing for conflict.

When the provisional government sent units of the regular army to restore order, these went over to the insurgents, who then declared the Commune. While Marx and his followers have claimed this as another installment of class war, others, pointing to the nationalist tone of the insurrection and the lack of specifically proletarian objectives or manifestations, have questioned his interpretation. In any case, the leaders, not to mention the rank and file, of the Commune were too varied to justify any single classification; but in comparison with the June Days, significantly more were Jacobin than proletarian. If one remembers that a large number of "workers" in 1848 came from the provinces and that Paris was isolated in 1871, this is perhaps not so surprising.

The Commune has, in fact, been taken to represent a deep distrust of the provinces by Paris and a reciprocal resentment of the Capital by the hinterland. But Gambetta's dramatic attempt to rally support for the beleaguered city, in its resistance to the invaders, was clearly intended to revive the fanatical Jacobinism that had galvanized the provinces and saved Paris and the Revolution in the crisis of 1792. Further, it will be remembered, the only serious internal threat to the authority of Paris during the Revolution came not from the "provinces" in the rural sense, but from the peripheral cities. And the latter, even though their social and economic orientation had been altered in the meantime, remained the principal foci of the urban capitalist society. As such, their latent suspicion of, and hostility toward, the administrative state and its Capital had survived to burst out in another episode of limited but savage civil war.

While Paris was under siege, representatives of the capitalist society were able to negotiate a cease-fire, conduct an election, and organize a provisional government—significantly at Bordeaux—to accept Bismarck's terms. The president, Adolphe Thiers, was not only a *protégé* of Talleyrand, but a supporter, albeit disgruntled, of the July Monarchy, an irreconcilable opponent of the Second Empire, and a wealthy businessman. With the machinery of the state at his command, he used regular army troops to reconquer Paris from the *Communards,* undoubtedly under the impression that he was repressing another class war of the 1848 variety. In retrospect, however, the fact that he re-established the government at Versailles, where it remained for nearly ten years, makes it apparent that he looked on Paris much more as an enemy city than the nation's Capital.

Once it had concluded peace with the Prussians and crushed the revolt of Paris, the National Assembly undertook the task of constituting a new regime. At the outset, the "monarchist" majority in the Assembly seemed to suggest the feasibility of a restoration. Although both republican and Legitimist polemicists have connived at building up this legend, each for their own political purposes, the possibility of such a denouement should probably never have been taken seriously. Perhaps the Legitimists, who were easily the least realistic politicians on the scene, had some illusions of bringing their candidate, the Comte de Chambord, back as king; but how serious the Orleanists were when they agreed to accept this aging, inexperienced grandson of Charles X, on the understanding that he would be succeeded by their Comte de Paris, is hard to gauge. In all probability, they did not want either on the throne. Having suffered from the equally unacceptable behavior of kings from both lines, these oligarchs seem to have been more interested in the constitution of a corporate executive, to run the state and protect their interests, than the restoration of any monarch.

By 1871 all established forms of government in France had been discredited: personal rule, not merely in its imperial but also its legitimist and presidential versions, was in disgrace; the Republic was distrusted because of the Jacobins' campaign to continue the War; and the parliamentary monarchy of the Orleanists was detested. The one remaining institution on which to build was universal suffrage. Not only did the electorate lack any political coherence, none of the traditional "party" labels, Legitimist, Orleanist, or even Republican, evoked any solid electoral support in the countryside. The Orleanists, however, still had the most experienced leaders, as well as the most highly developed sense of political purpose. By accepting the label of the Republic and at the same time offering security to the propertied classes, including the peasants, they were able to re-establish their corporate sovereign in the form of a parliamentary government. It was this compromise, conservative regime that in Thiers' famous *mot* proved to "divide France least"; but as Beau de Lomenie has demonstrated, its underlying purpose was to keep the administrative powers of the government from falling into hands hostile to the interests of the *grands bourgeois*.

The capitalist urban community, however, was not only still decisively outnumbered by the old agricultural society, but its internal class hostilities were sharper. The repression of the Commune and the execution, imprisonment, or exile of its leaders had undoubtedly retarded the political organization of the proletariat, but hardly lessened its hostility to the bourgeoisie. In any case, the only large and relatively stable electoral base was the peasantry, and there is evidence that the Orleanists were not only aware of, but ready to exploit this resource. Professor Sanford Elwitt has discovered that in the by-elections of 1873, urban money was invested in rural campaigns to press the charge that the "monarchists" intended to restore the church lands. The "republicans" who perpetrated this effrontery were, needless to say, of conservative (that is, Orleanist) complexion; and their efforts bore fruit in a series of electoral successes. At the same time, the true Jacobin republicans, having long since lost their hold on the agricultural society, as the peasants sank deeper and deeper into their post-Revolutionary conservatism, began to turn to the new urban proletariat for support. Gambetta's Belleville program was a precocious example of this trend, which, because of the widespread reaction against the Commune, lay dormant for at least a decade.

The plebiscitary potential of universal suffrage, however, was disarmed by the combination of a parliamentary executive with a highly centralized administration. Because virtually all local government was administered from Paris and the election of deputies was carried out in small, single-member constituencies that coincided with the basic administrative unit, electoral contests were bound to turn on local issues. And if this fact would inevitably make the organization and operation of national political parties difficult, it would by the same token serve the purposes of the *grands bourgeois* by tending to diffuse the power of the state. Political parties, as distinguished from political alliances, were formed within each society and tended to represent the Right, Left, or Center of one or the other. Since, by the end of the century, the new urban-capitalist France was nearly as large as the old agricultural community, no political segment of either could comprise much more than a quarter of the total electorate. Actually, the organized parties were seldom that large, and there was, therefore, no possibility of the parliamentary ministry being controlled by a single homogeneous party with a coherent policy. Majorities had to be put together by combining diverse interests in electoral or parliamentary alliances, more often than not, between parties from each of the two societies. Further, these arrangements were characteristically defensive, designed to oppose some positive legislation such as tax reform, which virtually everyone agreed was needed, but few were willing to accept. Inevitably such negative politics stressed local, rather than national, interests and gave the Third Republic its well-deserved reputation for *immobilisme.* They also involved the constant readjustment of forces, producing the notorious ministerial instability. Paradoxically, the two reinforced each other making the basic rule of government: *plus c'est instable, plus c'est immobile.*

The overriding challenge to aspiring politicians in the early years of the Third Republic had been the organization of constituencies. Since the introduction of universal suffrage in 1848, virtually all elections had been plebiscitary in character. Obviously the new parliamentary regime would require party organization, and that proved to be.a surprisingly difficult and time-consuming task. From the first, aspiring leaders realized that the peasants constituted the single most important bloc of votes, and the urban proletariat the second. The latter, however, was effectively disorganized for more than a decade by the repression that followed the Commune, leaving the former the only electorate worth systematic cultivation.

In the election of 1871, the issue was peace or continued resistance to the Prussians; and peasant votes were solicited by the rural partisans of each side, the small-town professional men for Republican defense and the landed gentry for the Treaty. The doctors, lawyers, teachers, and postmasters were intellectual positivists, anti-clericals, and Jacobin republicans; the resident nobility, by contrast, were normally pro-clerical, Legitimist, and conservative. The peasants, having little real interest in politics, voted for the *status quo* and, in spite of their lingering distrust of both nobility and church, most were ready to support conservative peace candidates who were royalist, against too radical or belli-cose republicans, thereby contributing substantially to the "mon-archist" majority in the National Assembly. But as the first by-elections proved, the peasants did not vote for a restoration.

Just how seriously the royalist deputies to the Assembly took the ludicrous farce of negotiations with the Legitimist Pretender, the Comte de Chambord, is difficult to say; but it seems at least possible that he clung to the issue of reviving the white flag of the Bourbons as a way out of what he was coming to realize would be an impossible position. With Chambord's departure, the decision to elect Marshal MacMahon President of the Republic may have been as much to get rid of the tiresome Thiers as to "keep the throne warm" for the Orleanist Comte de Paris who, it was agreed, would succeed the aging and childless Chambord as Pretender. When MacMahon tried to defend his monarchist trust—in the incident now enshrined in republican hagiography as the *"Seize Mai"* (1877)—by dismissing a too independent ministry, he learned in the ensuing election that he had no mandate for personal rule. The real issue, it should be noted, was not the Republic, as has been alleged, but constitu-tional government by a ministry responsible to the parliament. The republicans had apparently decided to accept parliamentary government in order to forestall a restoration; and the Orleanists, to forego a king in order to maintain their parliament. From then on, the Republic was an ambiguous and divided, but deeply entrenched, regime. Although election after election would be won in its "defense," the Republic was never in serious danger until the military defeat of 1940. The real issue was not its pro-tection but its definition and control: would it be Jacobin—and dedicated to the rights of man—or Orleanist—and committed to the defense of private property?

During the first two decades of the Third Republic, the overriding problem for all political leaders continued to be the search for, and organization of, reliable constituencies. Early in the eighties, as both the war and the Commune receded beyond immediate concern, the political climate began to change. The Orleanist, *grand bourgeois* elite, who had established their authority in the *Seize Mai* confrontation, were challenged by the more moderate Republicans of the administrative tradition of the intendants. A series of Republican ministries implemented policies that would alter the political orientation of significant segments of the population. The first was the expansion and laicization of education; and the second, the building of the "third railroad network," which took feeder lines to most towns of the hinterland.

Both programs were criticized, undoubtedly with some justice, as calculated attempts to "create" republicans. The new lay schools certainly fostered Jacobin ideology and are credited with having contributed to a new republican outlook among the rising generation. The railroads had a different sort of impact. The "third network" did, as was charged, introduce a large public-works program into the rural backwaters of the country intended to buy votes for the Republic; but it did much more. Because it brought most of the market towns of agricultural France into some degree of contact with the commercial world, it involved them in a new way in the country's politics. This development might be expected to have moved the peasants out of the old agricultural society into the capitalist economy *en masse;* but manifestly it did not, as the population statistics of the period attest. Although the total number of rural inhabitants began to drop at just about this time, the decline was almost imperceptible at first and, through the first half of the twentieth century, gained momentum at a surprisingly slow rate. This meant, first, that the land was being cleared of its subsistence population to make way for new commercial farms at a very gradual rate and, second, that the vast majority of the peasant population remained ready to defend its traditional way of life even, if necessary, by voting for monarchist candidates.

Republican doctrine in these years began to express genuine concern for workers' problems; and in the Chamber, Radical deputies introduced bill after bill intended to ameliorate the lot of labor by factory regulation and unemployment insurance.

Needless to say, these efforts produced little concrete achievement, but their rhetoric frightened the conservatives; and their ineffectiveness can only have alienated the workers. In any case, after a half dozen years of "republican" rule, "monarchist" candidates made a partial comeback in the elections of 1885. The Legitimists read these results as a revival of their fortunes, and even the Orleanist Pretender moved to get on the bandwagon by issuing a manifesto proclaiming that the restoration would be accomplished not by parliament, but by plebiscite. The Orleanists responded to this apostasy with vigorous denunciations of their titular leader, once again emphasizing the ambiguities inherent in the word "monarchy." Some political commentators, however, contended that the republican label covered even more serious contradictions. To illustrate both points, it is only necessary to turn to the strange episode known as the Boulanger affair.

Because General Boulanger was long used as a political bogeyman, his real significance has tended to be obscured. First brought to politics by a radical minister, Clemenceau, in quest of a republican general to serve as minister of war and distract attention from the unfortunate aberrations of one of the party's most prominent members, the flamboyant Boulanger soon began to attract too much public attention to suit his fellow cabinet members. Their misguided efforts to return him to his previous military obscurity served only to free him to run—successfully— in one by-election after another and launch a serialized plebiscite of dangerous proportions. His support came largely from the Left, especially the provincial workers, apparently in response to his promise "to sweep the rascals out." Recognizing themselves as the objects of this program, his recent colleagues denounced him as a traitor to the Republic and began to look to their defenses. It was not, however, as one of his more articulate supporters pointed out, *the* but *their* (that is, the conservatives' parliamentary) Republic that was under attack.

Once the regime appeared in trouble, the General received overtures from new and unexpected allies; Legitimist supporters of the Pretender began secret negotiations, in which they offered Boulanger an astonishingly large subsidy, obviously in the ex-

pectation that, willingly or not, he could be turned into a General
Monk. Clearly, the politicized General and the "legitimized"
Duke were pursuing the same goal of freeing the state from its
constitutional shackles and providing a new executive chosen by,
and answerable to, the people, rather than the financial establishment of the Orleanists and their assorted bourgeois bed-
fellows.

The fact that both of these adventurers could not achieve
their personal ambitions at the same time, that neither was remotely capable of the task he had undertaken, and that their
misadventure ended in ridiculous disaster does not alter its
significance. It was another example of that *Carlo-républicaine*
cooperation noted by Tudesq. And the "latent Boulangism" that
commentators have so regularly attributed to the French, often
as a moral flaw, is another way of referring to the same instinct for efficient administrative government and distrust of
parliamentary negotiations characteristic of both the Right and
Left of the hinterland. Inevitably, the country's political leaders
studied the *affaire* and responded to it according to their lights
and interests. The Orleanists saw not only that a restoration
would be politically impractical, but that it would be dangerous
to their parliamentary government; and with the other *grands
bourgeois,* they began to prepare a new electoral base for a
conservative republic. The Jacobin radicals, sensing hazards in
a new plebiscitary campaign that would attempt to exploit class
antagonisms for the benefit of the Legitimist Right, began to
develop a counterprogram based on the needs of the proletariat
and known as *Solidarité.* Thus, for quite different reasons, both
urban conservatives and rural radicals found their interests best
served by working within the system of the Third Republic, in
spite, for the former, of its republican style and, for the latter, of
its parliamentary government.

The issue around which the conservatives organized their
campaign was protection. From the days of the Liberal Empire,
industrialists had complained about the low tariffs, but those
among the capitalist establishment involved in shipping, railroads, importing, exporting, and banking were likely to favor
free trade. With the important industrial expansion of the 1880's,
however, the balance of interest and influence started to shift

to the protectionists who, by the end of the decade, began to sense the possibility of developing electoral support among the peasants. The extension of railroad feeder lines into the hinterland by Freycinet had brought a large part of rural France into reach of the capitalist economy. Although this did not transform all peasants immediately into commercial farmers, it did involve an increasing number in some degree of commercial farming without undermining their essentially subsistence way of life. Needless to say, this sort of operation could not possibly compete with the new industrial agriculture of America or the Ukraine, to take two obvious examples, with the result that the peasants were ready to respond to the protectionist propaganda.

Following Boulanger's fiasco and the royalist debacle in the election of 1889, the conservatives mounted a vigorous campaign in preparation for the next election. Among their leaders one of the most important and clearly most characteristic was Jules Méline, man of the East, textile lobbyist, and left of center—that is mildly anti-clerical, republican, and protectionist. Working extensively through the new agricultural societies and cooperatives that were springing up in the hinterland, he not only won support for the famous Méline Tariff that was to become the strait jacket of French industry; but, by cementing a peasant-capitalist alliance, he laid an important foundation for conservative republican politics. At the same time, the Radicals and Socialists were both attempting to organize the urban lower classes. In the election all three groups made important gains at the expense of the old monarchist Right. Taken as a whole, the results were a resounding victory for the "Republic," which now commanded an overwhelming majority in the Chamber. It soon became apparent, however, that the victorious "Republicans" were irreconcilably divided between their own Right, or capitalist, and Left, or Jacobin, factions.

The leader of the "radical" Left, Léon Bourgeois, was convinced that the class struggle could be resolved by updating the old Jacobin morality to take account of the social and economic injustices of industrial society. He was neither a socialist nor a revolutionary; but he was prepared to use constitutional (that is, parliamentary) methods to achieve substantial social legislation and to finance it by a graduated income tax. Because the complacent conservatives allowed themselves the luxury of in-fighting, Bourgeois suddenly found himself in a position to form a ministry; and with the unswerving support of the small group of Socialist deputies under the remarkable leadership of Jules Guesde, he appeared to be in a position to carry out his program. As a result, the conservatives were suddenly faced with a crisis of extraordinary implication. In 1895, a program of serious social legislation, supported by a graduated income tax, would have been considered revolutionary in any country; but for the French *grands bourgeois,* it loomed as sheer disaster.

To defeat Bourgeois' challenge, the conservatives were forced to resort to a vote of no confidence in the Senate and to turn the social-political issue into a constitutional confrontation between the Orleanist-parliamentary and Jacobin-republican traditions. Constitutional government, not merely monarchy, depended, as Montesquieu had recognized, on a second chamber. It reduced government from the Jacobin tradition of enlightened administration to the bourgeois practice of negotiation and accommodation. And although the Senate was not often to exercise its authority in such a dramatic fashion, it was to remain the symbolic check on Jacobin initiative throughout the life of the Third Republic. By a parliamentary manoeuver, the conservatives finally forced the Bourgeois ministry from office and formed a new cabinet of their own under Jules Méline. Because the forces in the Chamber were so evenly divided, he was instructed to hold the ministry at any cost to prevent Bourgeois' return to power before the next general election. Under these circumstances, the obvious tactic for the Radicals was to probe for any issue that might dislodge Méline. The first prospect they turned up was the case of a Captain Dreyfus, convicted of treason and transported to Devil's Island instead of being executed. To Jaurès, this immediately suggested bourgeois privilege, but other members of the Left soon learned that there was reason to doubt not only Dreyfus' guilt but the integrity of the military court that had convicted him. Attack from that side appeared even more promising.

Because the Ministry depended on the support of a small group of extreme rightists who were violent in their defense of the army, and because there was no obvious reason to suspect that an injustice had been done, Méline did not even dare to admit the existence of an issue. His public assurance that there "was no Affair" not only allowed the issue to develop into a national crisis of extraordinary character and violence but became a classic in the category of famous last words. The rest of the story is too well known to need repeating here. Méline was swept from office, but in the ensuing confusion the campaign for the income tax and social reform was completely lost from sight. For a brief period, the Legitimists and other reactionaries saw another mirage of power, the threat of which was all that was needed to distract the Jacobin rank and file from social reform and to rally them to the more congenial task of defending the Republic. Waldeck-Rousseau's famous government of Republican Defense was as much intended to protect bourgeois France from the Left as the parliamentary regime from the authoritarian Right; and Combes' great success in the election of 1902 revealed a new conservative alignment of political forces that was to prevail, with only occasional interruptions, for over half a century.

The cornerstone of the new electoral structure was the Méline tariff. With the peasants committed to protection, the conservative capitalists had a dependable majority, or more accurately "anti-majority," that would make any progressive social policy impossible. Although a number of *grands bourgeois* did run successfully for the Chamber or Senate, they did not need to provide their own majority because, under the new circumstances, the Radicals had ceased to be a threat. Ultimately dependent on rural votes, the latter were forced to accept the protectionist bias of the peasants; once they did, however, they found they could be elected on such traditional and irrelevant Jacobin issues as anti-clericalism and republican defense. Radicalism was reduced from a cause to a career, and in the process the administrative state, so feared by the capitalist conservatives, was transformed by the decentralization of power into an engine of political incoherence, an "anti-government." To understand this metamorphosis, however, it is necessary to re-examine the social structure of the country at the beginning of the century.

CHAPTER SEVEN

The Anti-Government and
the Anachronistic State

———•———

IT WAS not surprising that the fiscal-military state created by the monarchy to organize the subsistence agricultural communities of rural France into a nation survived into the twentieth century. During the nineteenth, it had developed an institutional momentum of its own and had demonstrated that it could be used for modern purposes. Indeed, at the beginning of the new century, the nation-state appeared to be the model for modern social-political organization. In France, however, it remained the governmental expression of the hinterland, which in turn maintained its characteristic agricultural economy well beyond its liberation from the limitations of transport that had originally shaped its way of life. But not only did this old and apparently outmoded agricultural society persist, its peasants continued to dominate French politics in alliance with the capitalist *grands bourgeois.*

To many analysts it has seemed inevitable that, with the completion of the local railroad networks, the peasants must have been integrated in the new industrial society; and undoubtedly, to some limited degree, most did participate in the commercial economy. What must not be lost sight of, however, is that, even if they sold some part of their produce to the markets of the other France, millions of them remained peasants. Most significantly, the density of rural population declined very slowly in most areas, proving that whatever contacts the peasants were making with the market, they were preserving both their traditional attitudes and their essentially subsistence way of life. The degree to which the problems of this transition still plagued the country's politics and economy in the 1950's and 1960's demonstrates that the old society had survived the railroad revolution and was alive and vigorous through the first half of the twentieth century.

During much of the same period, the oligarchs of the industrial society had been able to control, or at least neutralize, the power of the state and to prevent its use as an engine of anti-capitalist social reform. Their relative success had depended on their political alliance with the peasants, in defense not merely of property but of the economic *status quo*. Together they formed that now infamous "party of order" that took as its *raison d'être* resistance to economic progress. For a variety of reasons, this program was attractive to a majority of Frenchmen but to the industrial proletariat it was a *casus belli*.

Politics in France at the turn of the century were at once deceptively simple and bewilderingly complex. Based on relatively stable social and economic conditions, they seemed to reflect clearly defined class objectives; but in fact, they represented the interests of the two distinct social hierarchies defined in the preceding chapter: the industrial-capitalist society of the cities and the administrative-agricultural society of the hinterland. Moreover, each society was still split by the traditional lines of social cleavage, with rural France being divided into peasants, small-town bourgeois, and landed aristocrats; and the cities, into proletarians, tradesmen, bourgeois, and entrepreneurs. The growing number of *fonctionnaires*, both great and small, who inhabited the cities, however, repeatedly demonstrated their allegiance to the administrative society. This sizable group of city dwellers, taken together with the inhabitants of the small towns of 2,000–10,000 (shown as urban population in official statistics), gave rural France a definite electoral advantage. Thus, although the migration from country to city was accelerating, its rate was still too moderate to give any immediate promise of reducing the peasants' electoral preponderance or creating a proletarian majority in national elections.

By 1900, the French capitalist community was committed to an industrial economy. Along the northeast frontier, beginning in the early 1880's a new major base of heavy industry had been developed, capable of providing steel both for the completion of the national rail system and the expansion of the country's industrial plant and production. It was at this juncture that the industrialists, in alliance with the peasant electorate, had succeeded in erecting the tariff that effectively eliminated most imports, including food. Without this protection, French industry and agriculture would have been forced, by severe foreign competition, to modernize their methods and drastically expand their production or go out of business. Whether the country could have managed an adequate response to survive unrestricted competition need not be decided here; rather, it is necessary to note the consequences of the recourse to total protection. With the domestic market virtually closed, prices and profits could be maintained and wages and volume controlled. The effect of this situation was so to reduce incentives to expansion that the rate of industrial growth in France lagged far behind that of Germany or the United States.

The political implications of the situation can be read in its effects on the two largest groups involved, the peasants and the industrial workers. The former were entrenched in a traditional way of life which, if it provided satisfactions, failed on the one hand to develop a market for industrial goods and on the other condemned the urban community to dangerously high food prices. Obviously it was the workers who suffered the most from this anomaly, particularly since the controlled industrial expansion provided a weak labor market, thereby condemning them to remain too small a minority either to exercise effective political power or to impose their demands by direct action. What was worse, both its own expansion and the decline of the peasants were so slow as to offer no hope of a political reversal in the foreseeable future.

In the early years of the Third Republic, even before the new heavy industries of the north and east had begun to develop a mass proletariat, the radicals had tried to translate working-class resentment, rural as well as urban, into political action. Although undoubtedly doomed to failure, this effort did not appear either as hopeless or as superficial at the time as it does in retrospect. Not only was the Jacobin tradition of the Radicals genuinely egalitarian, it was also as anti-capitalist as it was anti-parliamentary. At least at the outset, there was no more reason to dismiss the doctrine of *Solidarité* as cynical than to charge Léon Bourgeois with insincerity. The weakness of his campaign was that, under existing circumstances, it had no chance of success. Not only would the peasant-Conservative alliance preclude a Radical victory at the polls but the tariff—on which that alliance had been formed—would prevent the industrial development on which the Radicals' social program would depend.

Much as Calonne a century before, Bourgeois hoped for a humane and generous resolution of a desperate social problem; but existing political forces were too strong, and he was no revolutionary. Indeed, Bourgeois' most important motivation was precisely the desire to avoid class conflict. When he lost his political struggle in the countryside, and with it all hope for his program of reform, he withdrew from the contest. The significance of this transition was lost in the confusion of the Dreyfus affair and the consequent inclusion of a Socialist minister in the government of Republican Defense. What was clear for all to see, however, was that by 1902 the Radicals who were elected in large numbers in support of Combes had abandoned *Solidarité* and class reconciliation for anti-clericalism and the separation of church and state. If as Radicals they had lost their social purpose, as ambitious politicians they had found an unbeatable issue for their provincial hustings. Moreover, because of the country's centralized administration, this ideological issue allowed these new deputies to concentrate on the local scene. There the traditional Radical concern with social justice was irrelevant. The *status quo* was taken for granted, and deputies were expected to occupy themselves with immediate local needs that could be served by personal intervention and the willingness to trade a vote for a favor from the right minister in Paris. If this approach lacked principle, its purpose was clear. It protected local interests, elected local Radicals, and produced the *république des camarades*.

In this setting, anti-clericalism can be seen for what it was. In spite of some unfortunate and essentially irresponsible excesses during the Dreyfus affair, church and state had cooperated reasonably well on national or international problems. Clericalism, particularly after the school reforms of the 1880's and the *Ralliement* of the early 1890's, remained a burning issue only in rural France. In village after village, the rival *notables* who organized local politics and vied for the peasant vote were, on the one side, the local lord or his protégé and, on the other, the resident doctor or lawyer. On Sunday, the faithful of each cause assembled either in the church or across the *place* in the *Café du Progrès,* each motivated as much by distrust of the enemy *en face* as devotion to his own true faith.

If peasant voters were generally unmoved by this mock heroic confrontation, they were as little sentimental about the church as about Jacobin social justice. In fact, once it was clear that the Radicals could be trusted to defend the *status quo* and attend to local needs, they were likely to be elected against aristocratic or clerical conservatives. With a solid majority of the electorate committed to the existing social and economic conditions, the centrifugal pressure increased, forcing more and more political activity into the local circumscriptions and their problems.

The largest segment of the population for whom this *politique du village* was clearly unacceptable was the urban proletariat. Although at first most workers followed the anti-clerical crusade of the radicals, before long they began to realize its irrelevance to their cause. Disillusioned by the *défense républicaine,* some turned from politics to direct action through the growing *syndicats* and others retreated to a harder socialist line. When the International meeting at Amsterdam in 1905 ordered the French dissidents to accept party discipline and abandon their policy of political cooperation with bourgeois parties, Jaurès and the other leaders complied. This reunification of the French Socialists was, however, more apparent than real, with perhaps half the rank and file remaining alienated proletarians in the Marxist sense. In general, these latter were workers in the larger and heavier industries who, in the long run, would become social revolutionaries. But aware of their immediate political weakness, they tended to favor "direct" action through strikes for such limited objectives as increased wages or reduced hours of work.

Those Socialists who maintained their political orientation were modern Jacobins at heart. Characteristically, they represented the vast force of minor state officials, including school teachers and letter carriers; although they claimed to be "revolutionary" in their aims, they were not enemies of their society. Like their leader, Jaurès, they believed not only in France, but also in the state that they served and intended to take over and run. It was no accident that they provided some of the most dedicated and patriotic leaders in the First World War, nor was there anything surprising in the fact that an impenitent Jacobin, Clemenceau, and an old rural socialist, Briand, were the ministers who dealt most vigorously and effectively with proletarian threats of a general strike in the years before the War.

From their first appearance as an organized party in the Chamber in 1893, the Socialists gained strength with each election until, in 1914, they constituted one of the largest political groups in France. Even so, they posed no immediate threat of mustering a majority either in the Chamber or in the country. French industry was growing at a moderate rate, and the basic political alignments in the country were shifting only gradually. In the meantime, the condition of the proletariat was deteriorating in relative, if not absolute, terms; and much of the difficulty could be attributed to the protectionist tariff system. Not only did it allow industrial expansion to be limited, thereby controlling the labor market through a scarcity of new jobs, but it kept the prices of all consumer goods, particularly food, at artificial levels. As a result, the workers were not numerous enough to wield effective political power, but too numerous, in relation to existing jobs, to exert decisive collective action. Their wages were at once lower and their living costs higher than those of other industrialized countries. In this situation their eventual alienation was inevitable.

With the support of most of the agricultural community, the bourgeois conservatives were well entrenched in their defensive position; but this "party of order," as François Goguel calls it, was not so much a party as an alliance based on a common interest in resisting economic change or social progress. Its negative character, however, gave it a marked tactical advantage over the opposing "party of movement." Not only was this latter composed of elements from both societies and, therefore, vulnerable to all the inherent weakness of a political alliance, but it was seriously outnumbered. Even worse, its objectives involved positive action, which required much greater coordination than the negative cooperation on which the conservatives based their defense. This compound weakness of the "party of movement," it hardly need be urged, went far to make the much deplored *immobilisme* the curse of the later Third Republic.

How long this *status quo* could have been maintained, if the First World War had not intervened, is impossible to say. On the eve of mobilization, the balance of political forces, social structures, and economic development was changing in France but at a rate that promised little immediate relief from the existing system. Industrial production was increasing steadily, and with it, the working force. This meant not only that the Socialists were gaining strength but also that the country's economic resources were multiplying. If this pattern had been allowed to continue for any extended period, it would have produced both the political will and fiscal base necessary to mount a serious social program. There are even those who contend that desperate capitalist politicians, fearing exactly this denouement, connived at provoking the War as a preferable alternative. This thesis would be as hard to disprove as to establish, but it need not be resolved here. Whether Raymond Poincaré and the small group of ministers, diplomats, and generals who managed French foreign policy and preparation for national defense in the last crucial period were, as they alleged, genuinely convinced that Germany was preparing a war of conquest or whether they were merely using this as an excuse for their own criminal search for an alternative to class confrontation does not alter the significance of the outcome.

The threat of war did not become a general political issue until the summer of 1914, and the opposition of the Left was by no means total. Even Jean Jaurès based his promise to block French mobilization with a general strike on the conviction that the German Socialists would do the same. Whether his faith in international cooperation was shaken before his death is a matter of doubt, and what he would have done, once he learned of the *Reichstadt* vote, is impossible to say. What is beyond question, however, is that the other major Socialist leaders supported the

French war effort with energy and dedication, and that the French army—necessarily including a large contingent of industrial workers—fought with a courage and devotion seldom if ever matched by a modern European people. Clearly proletarian alienation was not yet complete in France.

The impact of the War was another matter: the loss of life among men of combat age was appalling, and a large part of French industry was overrun by the initial German attack. Because there was no time to create new plants, the French were forced to turn to Britain and the United States for much of their matériel, with the result that the War seriously curtailed, rather than stimulated, French industrial development. Further, the decision to finance the war primarily by loans, both foreign and domestic, left France in a vulnerable fiscal situation following the Armistice. These factors added up to a serious economic, social, and political setback for the country, leaving agrarian France entrenched in its anti-government and the proletariat hopeless and desperate in its impotence.

In the immediate postwar years, the French were obsessed by the problems of stabilizing the franc and restoring the devastated areas. Both depended, at least in part, on enforcement of the Treaty terms, including Reparations, on a reluctant Germany. In spite of the traditional view that Poincaré's occupation of the Ruhr was an unmitigated failure, it did lead directly to the Dawes Plan and the Locarno settlement, providing the first possible base for European peace and, at least initially, easing the fiscal and political problems of the French. Ultimately, however, these measures proved even more advantageous for Germany and condemned France to a position of inferiority and isolation on the Continent.

During the same period, both the French Socialist Party and the national labor movement split on the issue of Moscow's leadership. Superficially the new Communist Party was an obvious response to the Russian Revolution; but it also brought into the open the old division between the state-oriented *fonctionnaires* and the *petits bourgeois* of the administrative-agricultural society, on the one side, and the industrial proletarians of the urban-capitalist economy, on the other.

The distressing story of French politics between the wars

can be properly understood only in terms of the mounting economic, diplomatic, and military pressure under which the country labored. French industry never regained its moderate momentum of the prewar period. Even though by 1929 production figures finally climbed back to the 1913 level, they then receded again with the Depression. This meant that there was not enough wealth or capacity to support an adequate social program at home or to conduct an effective foreign policy abroad. It also meant that the movement of population from the old subsistence to the new capitalist society was slowed, further postponing the possibility of political reform. In this hopeless impasse, local issues continued to dominate politics, party alignments disintegrated, and cabinet crises succeeded one another at an accelerating rate.

The situation was further aggravated by the rising expectation of the workers and the mounting fears of the bourgeois. The mass character of the War had made the class distinctions, taken for granted in the nineteenth century, unacceptable in the twentieth; and the Russian Revolution demonstrated that an alternative to bourgeois society existed. As a result, French workers became more militant and less effective. By splitting the Socialist Party in 1920 over the issue of Moscow, they destroyed any chance they may have had for unified and consequential political action. At the same time, the postwar inflation, by eroding the savings of the lesser bourgeoisie, made that numerous class increasingly resistant to social reforms that would raise taxes or wages. The political impact of this reaction could be seen not only in the growth of right-wing parties, but the increasingly conservative stance of the Radical Socialists.

During the second half of the 1920's, the French "enjoyed," if to a lesser degree, the hectic prosperity and false security that pervaded the democratic world. With the stock-market crash and the onset of the Depression, it even appeared, briefly, that industrial backwardness might actually save France from the general disaster. Instead, by moderating the impact, it prevented the salutary, if painful, readjustments that were a product of the crisis in more developed countries like the United States. Antiquated plants and subsistence farming were not eliminated but given a reprieve. Even the Popular Front, in spite of impressive reforms, failed to modify the economic structure of the country significantly. Paid vacations and the forty-hour week may have made life more bearable for the worker, but they did not increase his purchasing power. Similarly, the nationalization of the Bank of France may have deprived the *grands bourgeois* of an important political lever; but it did not make capital more readily available for industrial expansion. And the nationalization of the arms and munitions industries probably reduced the country's military preparedness.

If the Popular Front experience seemed to demonstrate what an alliance of the Left could accomplish, it quickly proved, once the euphoria of 1936 had been dissipated, how unstable such a combination was. Even to discuss the divisions of the Left was misleading, because the Communists and Socialists constituted the radical wing, respectively, of the two societies still coexisting in France. The Radicals and Socialists at least belonged to the same system, but within it, they represented very different groups. Much has been made of the failure of French democracy during the thirties, but given the economic conditions both at home and abroad, it is hard to see how a democratic government could have functioned. Any really adequate social or economic reforms would, by definition, have eliminated either the *raison d'être* or special privileges of large segments of the population. The real issue was not merely taxing the rich to help the poor, but rather liquidating the peasant farms, small shops, and antiquated factories of provincial France. Thorough reform by democratic action would have required most Frenchmen to vote themselves out of their particular existence.

It was much less difficult to find a majority to oppose a constructive measure than to support one. Under these circumstances, the centralized administration kept the parliament occupied with local issues; and even this limited business required increasingly frequent recourse to "decree powers." These were not, as was often charged, so much attacks on democratic government as mere attempts to protect ministries from the regular parliamentary harassment that made it all but impossible for them to carry out their administrative responsibilities.

As the 1930's wore on, the French were increasingly paralyzed by the approach of war. The subsequent debate over the causes of the fall of France is as much an exercise in futility as were French efforts to prepare for the inevitable onslaught. Whether they consciously faced the facts or not, they must have realized instinctively that they had neither the men, morale, money, or machines—let alone allies—necessary for an effective defense. In such a literally hopeless situation, action was not so much impossible as irrelevant. France disintegrated as it awaited the impending blow.

Following the military and political collapse and the German occupation of the northern half of the country plus the Atlantic coast, Marshal Pétain attempted to govern what remained from Vichy. Actual authority seems to have rested largely with local officials, especially the mayors of the bigger cities; but the pretensions of the Marshal and his State still hold a compelling fascination for anyone interested in modern France. The new device, *Patrie, travail, famille,* which replaced the revolutionary *Liberté, égalité, fraternité* on public buildings, was clearly intended to evoke the spirit of the peasant hinterland. And there is no question that the Marshal did, and to a surprising extent still does, command the loyalty of traditional and rural France. The main significance of the Vichy experience, however, would seem to be its nightmare quality of dramatizing the anachronistic fancies of one side of the nation's schizophrenic soul.

During the same war years the "other France" was also occupied by dreams, but these were of the future. Perhaps the most important achievement of the Resistance was the merciless reexamination to which it subjected the established bourgeois values of prewar France. Under the brutal conditions of the Occupation, the old materialism appeared utterly unacceptable, either in retrospect or in plans for the post-Liberation future. At the same time, the hardships of the period drove home to the intellectuals of the Resistance, most of whom were of bourgeois origin, the necessity of a minimum material base for a good life. They realized, moreover, that the moral redress they sought could not be effected by merely sharing the wealth of the rich among the poor, but that the country's resources would have to be developed to provide the food, shelter, and amenities that would make a civilized existence possible for all.

Quite another group of Frenchmen brooding over their country's plight—some from the vantage point of the United States—began to understand that none of these fundamental problems could be solved in purely national terms. France, they recognized, was no longer, as it had once been, a viable economic unit; and neither French industry nor agriculture could thrive in anything less than a European context. With their country under German occupation, they came to the conclusion that the only way to coexist with their captors, after liberation, would be to join them in building a common European community.

These two visions of postwar France may have been different, but they were complementary, and together, provided the outlines of a truly new and humane society. By their very newness, moreover, they challenged virtually all surviving vested interests or established patterns of existence. At the Liberation, the demand for a total reconstitution of French society, even if far from unanimous, appeared too powerful to be resisted; but as Albert Camus was to comment with increasing bitterness, the commitment to the Revolution was dissipated with each passing day. Even so, the political orientation of the country remained far to the left of the old inter-war norm.

The confused history of post-Liberation politics centers on a struggle for power—the first order of business was to establish a provisional government that could begin to deal with the immediate and urgent problems of restoring the badly disrupted economy and recreating a constitutional government. Both De Gaulle and the Communists had plans for the radical reorganization of the country. As President of the interim government the General appeared well placed to influence developments; but it was the Communists—as the largest and only disciplined party —who posed the greater threat. Beginning with a frequently sinister *épuration* in the provinces, they seized many local governments, infiltrated the central administration, and participated in the provisional ministry. Given their display of courage, energy, and purpose in the Resistance, as well as their obvious numerical strength, they could hardly have been excluded from an important share of power, and probably few Frenchmen would have thought they should be.

Another new political force, also "liberated" by its members'

Resistance record, was what came to be called the *Mouvement Républicain Populaire*. Led by liberal or even left-wing Catholics, the *M.R.P.* at first backed De Gaulle and demonstrated electoral strength comparable to that of the Communists. The third major political group was the old non-Communist, non-Catholic Left, represented by a revived Socialist party. Originally there seemed to be large areas of agreement between the three. All favored the vigorous exercise of state power to improve the management and distribution of the country's limited and disorganized resources; and to this end, there was a wave of nationalization of public services, banks, and other financial institutions, and even some major industrial plants. At the same time, the social services initiated by the Popular Front government were extended and reinforced in a way that not only moved France along the road to socialism but greatly expanded the role and strengthened the authority of her administrative government.

As the provisional Assembly attempted to draft a new constitution, however, fundamental differences began to appear. The one point of ostensible agreement was on the denunciation of the late Third Republic, but that common ritual did not provide a workable base on which to construct a reassuringly different Republic. French constitutional tradition suggested only two ways of avoiding the old evils of *immobilisme* and *instabilité:* the first being the elimination of the upper house and its veto power on the popular assembly, and the second, the creation of a strong president. Obviously De Gaulle favored the latter and the Communists the former. In the immediate post-Nazi period, however, the mere suspicion of personal (that is, dictatorial) power was unacceptable, even if the beneficiary were such a hero as the General. His wishes thwarted, he resigned and "retired," leaving the field clear for the new constitution in which power was concentrated in a virtually unchecked unicameral assembly. But no matter how well this document met the rhetorical preconditions of differing from the Third Republic while maintaining the "republican" tradition, it also began to look more and more like a permanent committee for *coup d'état*. As the unique instrument of sovereignty, it would be not merely a legislative, but also a constituent assembly, capable of rewriting or suspending the constitution in any given session. With the Communists within the reach of at least a temporary majority, the implications of such an institution began to trouble both the Socialists and the *M.R.P.*, who united to defeat the draft constitution in a national referendum.

To most observers, the revised draft that was ratified in a second listless referendum seemed to differ only slightly from the first—in fact, the differences were critical. By introducing a shadowy consultative upper house called the Council of the Republic, the new document actually revived the Senate and the parliamentary government of the Third Republic. If to many this denouement was as discouraging as it was unexpected, given the nature and power of the administrative state, it was the only available alternative to the dictatorship of either a party or a man. And before long, it became clear that the price of this escape would be the return to the old parliamentary *instabilité* and *immobilisme*.

Immediate postwar France of 1946 was neither as populous nor as prosperous as immediate prewar France of 1913. The social and economic organization of the country had changed remarkably little during the intervening years, which is to say that agriculture was still largely peasant and subsistence, that manufacturing methods and machines were antiquated, and that merchandizing practices were primitive. The old agricultural-administrative society had survived both wars and the Depression, if not intact, at least *en masse*. If France was to survive in any recognizable way—and that probably meant if Europe were to remain part of the West—the old society would have to be absorbed, not by the old capitalist economy, which still lingered, weak and vicious, but by a new national, or even better, European community capable of supporting its population without enslaving it.

How could such a new society be created? Recourse to a traditional nineteenth-century revolution was hardly practical in the mid-twentieth century, when outsiders could be counted on to intervene. If the French could have been assured that a "communist" revolution would not have involved a Russian occupation, the story might have been different. Unwilling to accept that price, they set out once again along the parliamentary path in quest of their elusive salvation. Marshall Aid and NATO made the effort possible, but not easy. Even with the vision, the resources, and the time to create their new society, the French had to agree among themselves which concessions and sacrifices each would make for the common good; and each had at least some misgivings or reservations about the personal implications of the peaceful revolution they were about to undertake.

As the Fourth Republic began its parliamentary life, the old party divisions reappeared, in a modified pattern and with some new names. The three large Liberation parties lost strength: the Communists gradually, the other two more rapidly. The old Radical-Socialists made a significant comeback, a new group of Independents emerged representing local conservative interests in the provinces, and in 1947 General De Gaulle launched his famous *Rassemblement du Peuple Français*. The Communists, Socialists, and Radicals represented much the same constituents they had before the War; but the other three were new. The *M.R.P.*, heirs of the Catholic Resistance, were neither a clerical nor a conservative party in any traditional sense, and at the outset frequently rivaled the Left in social views. They were, however, the principal proponents of Europe, NATO, and the defense of the Free World, which—in Indochina—lent them an imperialist complexion.

The *R.P.F.*, De Gaulle contended, was not a party but an alliance of men of vision and action who, regardless of political affiliations, were dedicated to the restoration of France. To a certain degree, it was composed of followers borrowed from other parties; but French observers were not slow to note that its rank and file seemed to be made up of Pétainists. This anomalous situation was usually attributed, with some justification, to the pathological fear of communism nourished by these ex-Vichyites. Nevertheless, the consistency with which most of the Marshal's devotees voted for De Gaulle, as regularly as they reviled him, even after the Communist danger had subsided, suggests some other explanation for this apparently unnatural alliance. In terms of the two societies, of course, both De Gaulle and Pétain obviously belonged to the right wing of the rural administrative system. Their irreconcilable animosity arose not from ideological differences—the General had been the Marshal's favorite protégé—but from personal, even filial, rivalry. Following Pétain's disappearance and De Gaulle's return, the old rural reactionaries found it necessary to swallow their personal antipathies if they were to vote for their traditional principles. From 1940 on, De Gaulle's purpose was constant: to establish his personal authority over France. Whether his basic motivation was subconscious and psychological or ideological and political need not be settled here. Only a revived and reinforced administrative government would suit his purpose, and given his lack of royal or imperial connection, that meant a presidential regime. He had no more trouble accepting the Republic, so long as he was its master, than had Bonaparte. But in the old *Carlo-républicaine* sense, he was both anti-parliamentary and anti-capitalist. It was this that separated him from his original Resistance supporters of the *M.R.P.* as surely as it bound him to his old enemies of Vichy. Finally, although he could count on most conservative peasants and provincial businessmen to vote for him in crises, as insurance against their *bête noire,* communism, they were far more interested in their own local affairs than the General's vision of a regenerated France. In fact, they were the heirs of the old Méline alliance and, as such, were still determined opponents of all economic and social change.

Between the reconstitution of the parliamentary Republic in 1946 and the mobilization of France for the Algerian War in 1956, the central agonizing issue was economic progress. The Communists, Socialists, and *M.R.P.*, each in their own fashion, were committed to the concept; the Radicals were divided by it; the Independents opposed to it; and the Gaullists willing to pay it lip service while they sabotaged it. Any implication that the idea enjoyed a political majority would be misleading because the Communists, committed to the seizure of power, voted in all but automatic opposition to every cabinet and the Gaullist objectives and methods were much the same. As a result, ministries were forced to assemble their majorities from two-thirds to three-quarters of the members of the Assembly. This situation produced two important results. First, it was impossible to construct a working majority either for or against social or economic progress—each succeeding government represented a subtly shaded compromise; and second, it was rare that a ministry could be held together for more than a few months. These two weaknesses so discredited the Fourth Republic that De Gaulle was able not merely to bring it down in the Algerian crisis, but to maintain himself in power for years by the mere threat of abandoning the country to the old "chaos."

Frustrating and demoralizing as the parade of compromised and impotent ministries was, however, the Fourth Republic had served the country well. What was too often overlooked was that in its early years a clear, coherent majority for economic progress would have had to deal with the country's *kulaks,* just as a majority for the *status quo* would have faced the necessity of mastering the workers. France was far too evenly divided, and also far too civilized, to have been able to resolve either problem with the dispatch that was demanded by the advocates of "efficient" government on either side. The accumulated effects of fifty or a hundred years' mistakes could not be rectified in five or ten, without unacceptable dislocation and suffering. In the early 1950's, it was all but impossible to realize that the old subsistence agriculture and the archaic industries were actually in the process of dying out. But stubbornly as the beneficiaries of this anachronistic economy defended their way of life, they were not reproducing themselves. The point was illustrated, if not proved, by the Poujade movement that swept France in the mid-fifties and seemed to symbolize her troubles. Observers were slow to notice that for all their passion and vigor these militant defenders of uneconomic shops were seldom under forty. Clearly, Poujadism was no more promising a career for the young than were the smaller peasant farms.

At the same time, the new France was beginning to take shape. The huge task of postwar reconstruction was primarily a government operation. Resources, including capital, were allocated by the state; and the use of Marshall aid, significantly, involved cooperation with other European states, thereby fostering the concept of international economic planning. From the very outset, French development was controlled by the small group of administrative experts that drew up the famous Plans. The Coal-Steel Pool with Germany and subsequently the Economic Community of Europe were developed by similar teams of *hauts fonctionnaires*. Industry itself participated in the process through its reformed and enlightened association, the once sinister *Grand Patronat*. Control of this organization slipped from the hands of the reactionary owners into those of a new breed of modern managers. While the details of this revolution are not relevant here, it should be noted that virtually the entire operation of reconstruction, reorganization, and development of the French economy within the new European framework was planned and directed not by businessmen nor even politicians but by administrators.

Given the size of the task, the limited nature of available resources, and the character of French tradition and education, no other procedure would have been practical; even so, this one did raise a fundamental question. If, in contrast with the disastrous reign of Louis XVI, France was finally saved by her intendants, would their very success serve to perpetuate the *ancien* (that is, administrative) *régime?* The obvious ability, dedication, and achievements of these men put any such consideration out of mind, at least while the Fourth Republic endured. What was seldom recognized was that that much maligned regime provided not only the best hope of progress, but also of humane adjustment. In spite of its lamentable public image, it managed to absorb the political pressures generated by substantial social and economic reorganization. The decisive achievements of the Republic include leadership in the creation of the European Community and the establishment of the new economic base that produced the prosperity for which De Gaulle so regularly took credit. Without the political flexibility provided by ministerial instability and the fiscal elasticity provided by inflation, France would have risked violent confrontations during this critical transition.

The collapse of the Republic was caused by its inability to cope not with domestic but colonial affairs. After the long, debilitating war in Indochina, it was confronted by the irrational dilemma of the Algerian revolt. The terrorist tactics of the *F.L.N.*

could be contained only by the use of torture, but while the former was ignored and even condoned by much of the civilized world, the latter caused a scandal at home and abroad. The obvious conclusion was that Algeria would have to be abandoned to the rebels; but to a large majority of Frenchmen, this meant an immoral betrayal of fellow Frenchmen. It was a conflict they were not allowed to win, could not afford to maintain, and did not know how to resolve—an impasse that should be more understandable to Americans today than it was then. The Republic literally crumbled under the mounting pressure; and De Gaulle seized the opportunity to bring himself to power. Promising, at least by implication, to save Algeria, he resolved the problem by a veiled and gradual surrender. By the time his intentions were clear, the French were ready to accept his *fait accompli* with a guilty and resentful sense of relief.

With the advent of the Fifth Republic came the first flush of prosperity. Not only did this fortuitous coincidence considerably ease the constitutional transition, but the unaccustomed phenomenon of a stable, effective government drew admiring approval. Finally, the early revaluation and stabilization of the franc was welcomed as a miracle after nearly half a century of continuous inflation. Not even the death throes of French Algeria seriously marred the political honeymoon in France.

The new constitution, endorsed with desperate indifference by national referendum in the crisis of 1958, seemed to many to be as innocuous as unnecessary. In spite of some obvious bolstering of ministerial and presidential authority, it looked surprisingly similar to the preceding version. Most politicians, at least outside the Gaullist camp, probably did not suspect that it would not allow them to return to essentially traditional, if slightly more disciplined, parliamentary politics after the emergency was over. In fact, shortly after peace had been established in Algeria, several non-Gaullist members of the Cabinet asked the General to clarify some of his disquieting references to Europe. His reply came in three installments: he accepted the resignations of his interpellators; he announced a referendum on a constitutional revision, transferring the election of the president to the national electorate; and finally—with the referendum passed and his position thus reinforced—he abruptly vetoed

Britain's bid for membership in the Common Market in most undiplomatic language.

This series of events can be read, on one level, as evidence of De Gaulle's determination to achieve personal power and to use it to settle old scores with *les Anglo-Saxons*. On another, however, it can be seen as the re-establishment of administrative government and the all but inevitable reversal of French policy in Europe. To protect the reinvigorated state from disintegration and merger in the new larger community, the General rallied the surviving adherents of the old rural society to its defense. In addition, he organized the bureaucratic elite and courted the still numerous small tradesmen and businessmen threatened by the rising tide of economic progress. By very tough political manipulation, facilitated by bitter divisions among his opponents, he was able to translate this support in the country into a rigidly disciplined majority in the Assembly, which made a mockery of traditional parliamentary government.

Although details of specific elections are not relevant here, it is necessary to point out that the key to an understanding of contemporary electoral mechanics in France is the Communist Party. Still a solid voting bloc, it had long since sacrificed its original but futile objective of total power to the more practical aim of building a self-sustaining bureaucratic structure. Dependent on a loyal, but by no means obedient, electorate, the Communist leaders knew that the greatest threat to their fief was a successful revival of the Popular Front that would break the Gaullist hold and move the country more rapidly on its course toward economic and social reform. François Mitterrand came close to carrying out such a coup in the 1965 presidential election. If Jean Lecanuet and his *Centre démocratique* had thrown their support to Mitterrand on the second ballot, he could have won. But Lecanuet, who had the most to gain from a Mitterrand victory, prevented it by his principalian refusal to back anyone supported, however reluctantly, by the Communists.

If Mitterrand had won and carried out his promise to reestablish constitutional (that is, parliamentary) government, much of De Gaulle's captive (that is, anti-Communist) support would have gone to Lecanuet, giving him the ministry. Far more important, however, such an upset would have moved French politics off the dead center of administrative rule. Instead, De Gaulle was able to consolidate his personal power; and with each step, his purpose and its logical consequences became more clear. If, during its first four years, the General's government was widely accepted as a significantly improved version of the Third and Fourth Republics, once the War was over and the popular election of the president had been established, it began to look increasingly like an updated successor of the Second.

In retrospect, it seems no accident that De Gaulle followed his constitutional coup with a veto on Britain's bid for admission to the Common Market. Only the first in a long series of rebuffs to the European Community, it should have been taken as a warning that the commitments, specific and implied, to merge French sovereignty in that larger whole would not be honored. The state, as De Gaulle revived it, and Europe, as an emerging entity, were mutually exclusive structures. Following his re-election in the first popular presidential poll, De Gaulle withdrew France from the North Atlantic Treaty Organization, though not from the Treaty itself. In practice, this meant removing French units from NATO command, and NATO units—particularly the American contingents and bases—from France. Assuming this was primarily an expression of his obvious hatred of the United States, it still followed the logic of his revival of the state. The armed forces had always been an integral part of that administrative system and would have to be brought back wholly under its authority.

Ridiculous as De Gaulle's new policy of national defense, with its pretense of a strategy oriented toward all points of the compass, clearly was, it did mean reorienting industrial and fiscal priorities. Not only did this readjustment squander money and materials, it reduced the country's capacity for healthy economic development. Even De Gaulle's critics, however, were embarrassed by the argument that whatever could be said against his foreign policy, the country was stable and prosperous with a remarkably hard currency and efficient administration.

To what degree the student revolt of the spring of 1968 was a direct attack on the administrative state is hard to say. Much of their rhetoric was directed against the entire establishment of bourgeois society; but, within that larger context, it was not hard to find intense resentment channeled against the General and his state in its various manifestations from the infamous *C.R.S.* (police) through the university to the subsidized theaters. In fact, their black flags of anarchy were probably far less nihilistic in symbolic intent than most bourgeois feared. Many of the student "free communes," maintained within the buildings they had seized, were orderly and efficient societies. Anarchy apparently involved opposition not to local self-government, but rather to remote institutional controls. The unprecedented response of the workers to the student initiative seems to have involved a similar reaction to administrative authority. The entire general strike produced only vague objectives and demands; and when the Communists and Gaullists connived at a quick settlement with substantial material concessions, it was rejected by the rank and file. Perhaps the most astonishing thing about the entire crisis was its spontaneity: its lack of organization, effective leaders, or stated aims. The professional politicians failed lamentably in their ill-inspired effort to assume control, and not even the much publicized student orators proved equal to the task of mastering events. In spite of student denunciations of the materialistic bourgeois society and the standard worker affirmations of class solidarity, there was no hint of class war. Violence was almost entirely confined to conflict with the police (that is, the state) and any "bourgeois" who ventured out after dark in Paris was in far more danger from them than from the students. The strikers were even careful not to interfere with the food supply or any other basic necessities. The enemy was not so much society as its institutional façade. When the government, at the point of losing all semblance of control, dissolved the Assembly and called for new elections, however, it at once became an unequal contest. Neither students nor workers had candidates, and for once the General's threat of "after me, chaos" had a convincing ring. An overwhelming majority voted against that vague but frightening alternative, but no significant portion of the population voted for him with any manifest enthusiasm.

The state had been indicted, challenged, all but swept away, and then reprieved; but what use it was to make of its borrowed time was a question to which the answer was to be "too little and too late." The strike, not to mention the student disruption, had put a severe strain on the economy in general and the treasury in particular. One apparently obvious consequence could be the devaluation of the franc, but the General deftly side-stepped that issue. By postponing the day of reckoning, he allowed the situation to deteriorate beyond any palliative solution. Not only did this necessitate the revaluation of the mark, it also demonstrated the essential interdependence of European currencies, serving notice that an independent national fiscal policy was no longer possible for France. As De Gaulle himself had often warned, the end of fiscal independence would mean the end of national sovereignty and the beginning of a European government. In the light of this conclusion, De Gaulle's revival of administrative rule and the consequent reinforcement of the state can be seen only as a foredoomed and dangerous aberration.

Just how the outworn institution of the state can be dismantled and replaced would be difficult to predict. With the nineteenth-century capitalist society dissolving almost as rapidly as the old subsistence agricultural one is disappearing, both will have to give place to something new. Present indications suggest the need of more general European and more local regional patterns of political and social organization to match the new decentralized but international economy that is taking shape. In this period of accelerating and bewildering change, the French instinct to cling to the traditional appears as strong as it is dangerous. Institutions, like the administrative state, can serve, but not preserve—nor, for that matter, long survive—the societies from which they grew.

Looking back over the two millennia since Caesar first created Gaul from its three parts, it is possible to trace the development, within that territory, of a series of socio-economic structures and their governmental institutions. Among these, the monarchical administration developed to organize the subsistence agricultural society of the fifteenth century was undoubtedly the most impressive. Today, with its last social and economic roots finally withering away, it stands a hollow monument to the survival power of institutions. The monarchy is finally dead, *Vive la France!*

Conclusion

———•———

THIS ESSAY grew out of efforts to explain how and why two essentially separate societies could coexist in the one apparently unified nation-state of France. To describe and account for this phenomenon, however, I found it necessary to develop theoretical models within the geographical setting of an abstract prehistory and the historical ancient world. These concepts not only facilitated the task but suggested an unconventional approach to historical analysis that, if valid for France, should—with appropriate adjustments—be applicable to other periods and fields. Because I first saw the problem of "the other France" in terms of contemporary politics, it was natural to explore its ramifications in the context of existing French society. But this exercise provided little enlightenment until the France I knew was not only reviewed in historical depth but examined in geographical perspective as well. Seen in this concrete form, the small towns of the hinterland suddenly revealed their essential economic, and therefore social, isolation.

Starting with Professor Lévi-Strauss' proposition that primitive societies developed within established patterns of the exchange of goods, wives, and messages, it seemed reasonable to assume that historical societies would also take shape within some similar sort of structures and continue to grow in complexity and size. Following this clue, I attempted to sort out the possible areas and patterns of economic exchange and social communication. Careful consideration of the geographical factor suggested that the exchange of goods, unless water transport was available, would be severely restricted and that the economic units of inland agricultural societies would remain the peasant village or, at most, a cluster of villages around a market town.

The exchange of messages, particularly in the form of military commands, on the other hand, would be limited only by major geographical barriers such as oceans or mountains or great distances. In such situations, feudal or monarchical authority could be extended over wide areas. When prevailing weapons were cheap and campaigns not too distant, peasant armies would be effective; but if weapons became expensive or military operations remote, some form of feudalism would be likely. Feudal monarchs, when they did emerge, would have great difficulty in mastering the disintegrative forces in their situation unless they could modify the pervasive subsistence agriculture of the hinterland sufficiently to finance a royal administration and professional army. Even though the difficulty of transport severely limited the exchange of goods, it was found that a monetary, or more accurately a fiscal, economy could be established by circulating money and men through a system of market towns and regional capitals. By this device, the subsistence economy could be made to support an administrative monarchy.

If this model seemed to fit much early French experience and even promised to account for the bifurcation of the original agricultural society into two rival systems—feudal and fiscal—it did not bear any resemblance to the Mediterranean society in which, Henri Pirenne insisted, the Merovingians had participated. The discovery of Pirenne's famous error in dating the Moslem conquest made it clear that the Carolingians had turned inland and north for some other reason and raised the question of the nature of the relationship of the Mediterranean to the hinterland. The classic example of Mediterranean economy was obviously the Aegean society of the sixth to third centuries B.C. Composed of cities, or city-states, with limited possibilities for inland expansion, this community used water transport to increase its production by specialization not only in crafts but also in plantation farming frequently based on slavery. In spite of the fact that these ancient Greeks have been much censured for their failure to unite in a proper state, they obviously thought of themselves as a distinct community—and a superior one at that—particularly in comparison with their neighbors, the Persians, who operated a vigorous territorial administration.

Once it is recognized that the Aegean cities participated in an active exchange of goods and messages, it becomes apparent that they represented a distinct type of social organization that differed strikingly from the characteristic land based kingdoms and empires of the time. Where the latter were rooted in subsistence agriculture, the Greeks lived by commerce which, by greatly fostering the division of labor, produced not only a higher standard of living but monetary wealth as well. With this pattern established, it was easy to recognize that other commercial societies, exhibiting similar characteristics, could be found in the annals of the West. Further reflection suggested that the two general categories of social organization—subsistence and commercial—had little normal contact with one another. By definition, subsistence economies were neither consumers nor producers of commercial goods, and the basic business of port cities was with other port cities or coastal plantations. One society was almost entirely oriented toward the land, the other largely to navigable water. But of course the littoral, on which the cities flourished, was usually also the periphery of the land mass that supported the agricultural monarchies. This meant that the wealth of the commercial societies was a constant temptation to the neighboring military states.

Under favorable geographical circumstances, port cities could defend themselves, as the Greeks did against Xerxes, but even when they succumbed to a land power's military authority, they were not usually integrated into its economy. The relationship was awkward at best and led sooner or later to revolt. Rome, however, offered an apparent exception to this rule. Originally an agricultural state with a tough peasant army, it conquered first the Italian peninsula and then the entire Mediterranean shore line, thus possessing itself not merely of a number of coastal cities but a complete commercial society. In this position, Rome could siphon off much of the profits without interfering with the operation of the commerce and, by using this unprecedented income, develop the largest and most efficient professional army yet known. Under the command of Caesar, its legions conquered half of what we now call Europe, including England, and for the first time brought its hinterland into direct contact with the Mediterranean. For a while, at least, the Empire gave the appearance of a single unified society. But even the Romans could not subdue geography. The unity of their Empire was military, administrative, and fiscal, but not economic. The indigenous population of the hinterland continued in its subsistence way of life; and the one important link between the two systems was the seemingly endless supply of slaves that the Roman conquests provided to work the ships, plantations, and shops of the commercial society.

When the frontiers had to be defended instead of extended, however, the source of slaves dried up; the commercial wealth, for this and other reasons, declined; and the inland administration decayed. What the Carolingians found, when they took over from the Merovingians, was not merely that their Mediterranean cities were not producing enough income to support a standing army but that their new heavy cavalry, with which they were to establish their power, could not be supported by money. Instead, it required land, a fact that turned the Carolingians to the rich valleys of the North.

The history of Europe as an independent and coherent society—not merely a hinterland of the Mediterranean world—thus began with Charles Martel. Even though commerce never wholly disappeared from the Mediterranean, France, when it took shape under the Capetians, was composed of a congeries of subsistence agricultural communities defended and dominated by a feudal warrior class. Not only was there virtually no trade, there was very little money in circulation in the interior. The king himself was merely a noble, even if the first, among other nobles many of whom were more or less his equals in every respect but title. To manage great fiefs, let alone entire kingdoms, without resorting to reinfeudation, however, required money to support an administration; and the feudal monarchs struggled incessantly to develop revenues for just this purpose.

By the end of the twelfth century, the circulation of money had significantly increased; and the monarchy, though still feudal, was developing a fisc. New towns, able and generally disposed to finance the king as the only agent of law and order, began to change the nature of the monarchy. That this urban development coincided roughly with the revival of trade in the Mediterranean and its gradual extension across Europe to the Baltic is a matter of record. Traditionally, the two phenomena have been considered closely interrelated. But the restoration of the geographical dimension to the historical account suggests that the connection was not only slighter, but far less casual, than has been supposed.

The royal towns were characteristically market centers; and the more famous commercial cities were not only to the east of the French monarchy but managed to resist conquest by, and integration into, any royal administration for a surprising length of time. This is not to say that the new towns did not support the monarchy but that they did so, not from the profits of commerce, but by generating small monetary surpluses from their local agricultural communities. Thus the process that transformed the monarchy, by providing it with a solid fiscal base, only modified the existing economic system of the hinterland societies. If this marginal participation by the rural towns in the country-wide fiscal economy increased their production slightly, it did not destroy their subsistence character.

As the new system took shape, the king was gradually metamorphosed from a feudal into an administrative ruler who, although he no longer depended on the services of his vassals, was nevertheless not yet able to reduce them to the status of subjects. Indeed, they continued to maintain sufficient independence to constitute a separate society which not merely coexisted with the new monarchy but competed with it for support from the same agricultural base. By maintaining their hold on the provincial courts, as well as much of the machinery of local government, they were able to defend their position until the Revolution. Their judicial authority constituted, as it always had, their government, just as the king's administration comprised his.

Concurrently with this development in France, the trade that linked the Mediterranean and the Baltic began to be diverted from the river valleys of western Germany to the Atlantic, leading to the discovery of the New World and creating a new Atlantic community that was destined to add still another element to

Europe's social composition. The new ocean commerce rapidly dwarfed that of the Mediterranean. Because its distances were greater, its ships were bigger; the lush plantations of the Caribbean were worked by an apparently inexhaustible supply of slaves from Africa; and the volume of trade handled, and profits reaped, by the new port cities along the North Atlantic coasts, including those of France, vastly exceeded anything ever known before. Inevitably the new monarchies attempted to share in this bonanza through control of their port cities; and while these latter often resisted, they were not usually able to establish or maintain their independence in the manner of their ancient Greek or medieval Italian predecessors. Although it is recognized that the Atlantic cities traded largely with one another, according to the classic model, and did relatively little business with the hinterland, the possibility that they constituted a coherent Atlantic community, or civilization, has already been considered and, perhaps prematurely, rejected. The hold of no king on his ports was broken, at least until the American Revolution, and no European power was strong enough to subdue the entire Atlantic littoral as Rome had that of the Mediterranean; yet if no single state could take over the Atlantic community, there is the alternative possibility that it took over several states. Reread in this light, the six revolutions of the mid-seventeenth century acquire a new significance. If merchant-class revolts in Barcelona, Naples, and Bordeaux were supressed, others in Portugal, the Low Countries, and England not only succeeded but supported one another, raising the question of whether or not they were establishing a common *pied-à-terre* for an emergent commercial society.

Bordeaux, Nantes, and other Atlantic ports of France continued restive and rich down to the Revolution. Even though they were garrisoned by troops of the monarchy, their interests attached them to the commercial community. In this essay, however, it is their relation to, and effect on, France that is under scrutiny. If their economic ties with the hinterland were inconsequential, their financial relations with the royal government were not. Oddly, the monarchy never learned to tax them effectively; but it didn't really need to because the great merchants were eager to supply even larger sums in loans. Commercial societies normally produced more profits than they could reabsorb; and administrative monarchies were chronic consumers of capital. In fact, in early modern Europe, royal treasuries were almost the only institutions capable of paying interest on capital in the amounts the merchants needed to invest—at least for a time.

In eighteenth-century France, however, the profits were too large and the monarchy too inefficient, with the result that the debt finally exceeded what the royal revenue could support. It was this imbalance that produced the fiscal-constitutional crisis that touched off the Revolution. In the final showdown, three groups: the monarchy, the nobility, and the financial (that is, the commercial) bourgeoisie were in irreconcilable conflict. Their attitudes and actions, if consistent with their respective ways of life, differed so strikingly from one another as to reinforce the thesis that they derived from three distinct societies, with systems of communication and exchange that overlapped or interacted only occasionally.

In a few months, the Revolution liquidated the old aristocratic society, together with its remnants of judicial government and privileges. Because the king had proven hopelessly incompetent in the crisis, the revolutionary leaders were forced to seek some form of national salvation through parliamentary action. In that undertaking, representatives from the port cities played a decisive role. Clearly, they understood the mechanism of such government better than their colleagues from the monarchical hinterland; but, by the same token, they did not understand the needs and wishes of the subsistence society that constituted the bulk of France. As a result, their constitutional efforts were frustrated; and when they blundered into and mismanaged a foreign war, they were swept from power by an aroused "nation," convinced its Revolution was in danger.

The ensuing Terror was the by-product of efforts to restore the old royal administration that had been dismantled in the first phase of the Revolution. Communications between Paris and the provinces were re-established by the central Committee of Public Safety, working through the local Jacobin clubs and reinforcing the authority of their messages by the threat of the guillotine. The work of modernizing the monarchical apparatus—which had been the objective of the pre-1789 revolutionaries—was completed by Napoleon. His Empire was based firmly in the agricultural society of the *ancien régime*, but organized in a vastly more efficient version of the old royal fiscal-military economy. Unfortunately, like his great royal predecessor the Emperor loved war too well; but before he was destroyed by his military ambitions, he could boast that he had eliminated the "other France" and united the nation once and for all.

Indeed, the records make it appear he had. Not only did his administrative and judicial reforms integrate the hinterland; but the Continental System, even if it did not eliminate all commercial relations with the Atlantic community, effectively terminated French participation in its affairs. During two decades of war with England, French ports stagnated; and the great merchants faded from public view. But a new group of bankers emerged to finance the armies of the Republic and the government of the Empire; and when Napoleon abdicated, it was they who arranged the transition to the Restoration, which they obviously believed to be the regime that would least threaten their investment in the state.

With peace, French ports re-entered the Atlantic commerce, but on a very different basis than before the War. During the period of the Revolution in France, the British had carried out their Industrial Revolution and, with effective control of the seas, had established a commercial superiority—flooding the coastal cities of the world with cheap manufactured goods—that was not to be challenged by anyone for a century, and never by France. Until railroads reduced the difficulties of inland transport, moreover, this commerce achieved only a limited penetration of the hinterland in France or elsewhere.

Instead of consumer goods, the French began to import machinery and to develop small mills throughout the interior: some located near raw materials but others near the waiting markets of towns and cities. Some of the goods produced circulated surprisingly widely, but most must have been locally consumed. Collectively these scattered industries represented a considerable investment and employed a growing labor force; and by the mid-nineteenth century, constituted a new industrial society complete with capitalist entrepreneurs and alienated workers. This history of the next century was the story of the symbiotic relationship of the two, coexisting in the same nation-state. The refusal of the older France to die, and of the other to come of age, left the country politically schizophrenic, accounting for the chronic incoherence or irrelevance of its various regimes. Just when the new capitalist communities first constituted a discrete society, "another France," is hard to date. Even though the Restoration had been arranged by bankers, it still appeared to be a modern version of the old administrative monarchy. The July Monarchy, however, manifested many characteristics of a mature capitalist society: not only was it ruled by oligarchs; but it produced an industrial proletariat and, with its fall in 1848, brought the country's first outburst of modern class war in the June Days.

By parliamentary manipulation of the National Assembly, the same oligarchs made a half-hearted attempt to turn the Second Republic into another bourgeois regime. The reason for the easy acceptance of its violent transformation into the Second Empire was similar to that of its more illustrious prototype: a widespread desire to lend the Republic greater coherence by establishing a plebiscitary executive. Needless to say it was the government of, and for, the agricultural society, just as the Third Republic, in its turn, was the result of an attempt to revive the July Monarchy without a king. The problems faced by the new bourgeois republicans were complicated, however, by the introduction of manhood suffrage and the consequent possibility that the government might be captured by a combination of Jacobin republicans from the rural towns and the radical workers of the cities—a threat that was forestalled at the end of the century by an alliance of the capitalist entrepreneurs and the peasants. Based on a common interest in tariff protection, this coalition controlled the government and maintained the economic and social *status quo* until the Popular Front victory in 1936. It was during the same period, it should be recalled, that the oligarchs of the Third Republic first established the myth that their parliamentary system was the only truly republican form of government and then succeeded in defending it against the incessant attacks of both anti-parliamentary Jacobins and anti-republican monarchists.

Defeat and occupation in the Second World War shocked many Frenchmen into serious efforts to modernize their country by merging it in a new European economy. If the Fourth Republic was simply a restoration of the Third, the balance of potential forces had altered sufficiently to permit it to move steadily, if not spectacularly, toward the country's postwar goals. Since progress meant absorbing the old subsistence society into a new industrial one freed of the selfish control of the entrenched oligarchs, resistance was widespread and stubborn. Because the regime was unable, as well as unwilling, to liquidate its obsolescent but numerous opponents, it was denounced as ineffectual and swept away by the apparently insoluble crisis in Algeria and the ruthless ambition of Charles De Gaulle, just as it was on the threshold of success.

Although the constitution of the Fifth Republic promised a more disciplined form of parliamentary government, the General intended to transform it into a presidential monarchy in the old administrative tradition. If his resolution of the Algerian impasse had at first suggested that such a regime might have its uses in the modern world, his subsequent sabotaging of the Common Market clearly demonstrated that it did not. The revolt in May 1968 seemed, more than anything, to be against the anachronistic institution of the administrative state and its personification in the General.

The conclusion of this essay is not merely that modern France is still comprised of two identifiable and discrete—if obviously decaying—societies. Rather, it is that the rereading of French history in geographical perspective greatly facilitates the identification and description of the social and political structures that have developed in that country. This conclusion also carries the implication that comparable socio-economic organizations must exist, or have existed, in other times and places, producing their complicated patterns of governmental control of the territory they inhabit. Further, this study suggests that preindustrial societies tended to fall into one of two general categories: those based in subsistence agriculture and those living by water-borne commerce. While endless variations can be found within structures of either type, the principal distinction remains that between land and water orientation. An agricultural society with feudal institutions can develop a feudal and then an administrative monarchy—but not a commercial economy. It is worth noting, moreover, that the distinction between the agricultural and commercial societies is not simply that of town and country. If the commercial is largely urban, the agricultural also produces cities, occasionally great ones. But its monarchical capitals or local administrative centers are very different from commercial ports.

The analytical concepts and techniques outlined here can be further developed in two different directions. They can, of course, be used to analyze other major areas or periods of history; but they can also be turned to the close scrutiny of the components of any self-contained social structures. In the first category, as has already been suggested, the English Revolution might be reread as a struggle between members of the new commercial society—that was coming into existence in the seventeenth century—and the old continental type of administrative monarchy—that still survived from earlier times—just as that of colonial America has been related in terms of the rivalry between inland settlers and Atlantic merchants. Similarly, it would be easy to see in contemporaneous Russia and Prussia the emergence of other classic examples of the monarchical state based on subsistence agriculture and organized by a fiscal-military administration. Indeed, this description might appear so obvious as to be uninteresting, at least through the eighteenth century.

In the case of Russia, however, if it is carried on into the later nineteenth and earlier twentieth centuries, it will suggest that the underlying motivation of the Bolshevik Revolution was the need for administrative reform in much the same way as it had been in France at the end of the *ancien régime*. The peasants swept away the nobles who had been their tormentors in residence; but the new "Jacobins" were, like their predecessors, bent on modernizing, not destroying, the machinery of central government. Also as in France, the urban proletarians were used as shock troops, especially in the Capital, to seize the seat of power. Seen in this perspective, the more recent development of heavy industry will appear a spectacular extension of the old fiscal-military economy. The result is not "state capitalism," as has often been charged; in capitalist terminology, it is a "classless society." Industrial capitalism, with its class structure, was a negligible factor in pre-1917 Russia and left no trace, for better or worse, in Russian attitudes or values. If Soviet citizens are human enough to enjoy their gradually rising standard of living, they look to the state to produce it; and to them, the state is still a military chain of command.

The history of Prussia during the same period offers a variation of the same theme. The monarchy of Frederick the Great was as far superior in administrative efficiency as it was inferior in size to that of his fellow despot, Catherine II. The famous *mot* that most states had armies, but that the Prussian army had a state was merely another way of saying the same thing. Not only were all administrative monarchies military in character, but the army was an essential element in their fiscal economies; and because of its unmatched efficiency, the Prussian army was larger in proportion to its population base than any other. Like all such regimes, moreover, it was both territorial and expansionist. This meant that when the unification of Germany became an issue, the Prussian military administration was the only existing agency capable of realizing that objective; but even the Wilhelmenian Reich dominated rather than organized the national territory. The Weimar Republic moved slightly away from administrative integration, and in reaction the Nazi Revolution was basically a drive for *Gleichschaltung*. The reason the army tolerated Hitler was not because of its much advertised anti-communist phobia but because of its fundamentally anti-capitalist orientation. The officer corps, as it demonstrated repeatedly, had no basic antipathy to a "communist" military state. What they did distrust was capitalist society and all its classes, including the proletariat. Hitler's objectives were essentially the same, if superficially an absurd caricature of those of the High Command. Some officers questioned his methods, most detested his style; but few differed with his aims. Thus they not only followed his orders, many even accepted the Nazi Party, because—like that of the Jacobins in 1793—it served to improvise a central administration by the threat of terror. Today, with Prussia safely behind the Oder-Neisse Line, Western Germany enjoys both a prosperous capitalist society and a federal government.

The possibilities of turning this technique of analysis to the close scrutiny of the internal structure of societies can be readily explored by returning to France. Not only the peasants but the provincial nobles, small-town bourgeois, and administrative *cadres* all constitute sub-structures of this society. At first glance it might appear that they had already been more than adequately studied and hardly required reconsideration even in a new perspective. Certainly the French need yield to no one in their preoccupation with sociological introspection; but anyone who has followed French politics since the Second World War will realize that the professional intellectuals of Paris, whether academics, journalists, or politicians, have repeatedly demonstrated surprising ignorance of their fellow Frenchmen of the hinterland.

The nobles, or more correctly the landed gentry, have been exhaustively portrayed in literature and the cinema; but how thoroughly they are understood as an element of the monarchical-agricultural society is unclear. Their generally disturbing reaction to the Dreyfus affair and puzzlingly stubborn attachment to the atheistic *Action française*, even after its condemnation by the Pope, might be reread as a deeply rooted commitment to the administrative state and instinctive suspicion of capitalist society, rather than mere perversity of character. The peasants, too, have been much written about and even scientifically investigated, but they remain a mystery to most urban Frenchman. The economic necessities of subsistence farming are frequently interpreted in terms of a romanticized mystique of the soil or an ugly form of avarice; and now that the last generation of peasants, as distinguished from commercial farmers, are dying out, their true character may be lost in a haze of vague nostalgia.

The small-town bourgeois—particularly as he comes to Paris to make his mark or fortune— also appears to be better known than he really is. Striking evidence of this was provided by the gross miscalculation of politicians and political analysts alike of the nature and strength of Poujadism in the middle 1950's. And finally, although there have been studies of prefects and various other categories of *fonctionnaires,* public servants from lowest to highest ranks are seldom treated as a single group. Yet, their inevitably disproportionate concentration in Paris might well be taken to explain the strikingly different voting patterns of the capital and the great provincial cities. In recent years, the bourgeois *arrondissements* of Paris have voted almost always for Gaullist candidates, that is in support of the administrative state, while the larger provincial cities have almost as regularly elected mayors that were economic (that is, capitalist) conservatives.

As this book goes to press, the most recent and most serious challenge to the Gaullist establishment has begun to gain momentum in a campaign for the decentralization of state authority in new, genuinely political—not merely administrative—regions. What the future of this particular movement will be is less important here than the evidence it offers that the significance of the state—not merely for the future of France but of Europe and the West as well—has finally been recognized and translated into a major political issue. But if the formulation is new, the problem it presents is not. Even if the specifically nineteenth-century version of the "other France" is now itself out of date, its struggle against the state takes on new interest in the light of the present context.

To any who questions its character or existence, I offer my discovery—made during an early Sunday morning stroll in the Place de la Concorde—that I was in the middle of an explicit, if tacit, monument to "the other France" and one of its short-lived triumphs over Paris and the state. The central focus of that beautifully organized space, as every tourist knows, is an Egyptian obelisk. Close inspection of a non-hieroglyphic inscription on its base will further explain that the considerable engineering feat of erecting it on its present site was worked out by none other than Louis Philippe. Why that Orleanist "King of the French" should have taken such a personal interest in placing such a huge and incongruous monument in the center of the two grandest vistas of his capital aroused by curiosity, and I recalled that it marked the location of the revolutionary guillotine and the execution of Louis XVI. Surely not a pagan monument to the martyred "son of St. Louis"! And then I remembered that the latter's faithful followers had vowed that on their triumphant return from emigration, they would erect an expiatory chapel on the spot where he had died. Clearly, Louis Philippe, son of the regicide Philippe Egalité, had blocked that project. I then looked up to find eight pairs of large unblinking eyes fixed on the obelisk. Could it be an accident that the eight heroic female figures representing the eight great peripheral cities—Bordeaux, Nantes, Brest, Rouen, Lille, Strasbourg, Lyon, and Marseille—that surround the Place, were stationed there to gaze with eternal fascination at the spot of Bourbon martyrdom? It was not. Together with the fountains dedicated to river and ocean commerce, they were, I soon confirmed, erected at the order of the same bourgeois King. If his personal triumph was short-lived, his monument to his "other—urban, commercial, and capitalist—France" has survived in the heart of Paris.

Index